Object Oriented Analysis & Design Cookbook

Introduction to Practical System Modeling

Edwin Mach

Cminds

Cover Illustrations: Edwin Mach
Author: Edwin Mach

ISBN13: 9781670943163

DEDICATION

This book is dedicated to my children.

When you put *your mind* to it, you can do *anything*.

(Additional Dedications towards end of the book)

[This page left intentionally blank]

OOAD Cookbook:
Introduction to Practical System Modeling

EDWIN MACH

CONTENTS

FOREWORD

I've been teaching Object Oriented Analysis and Design for over a decade and was compelled to write this book because the textbooks that I had been using in my class – students disliked it.

Nearly ten years later, I found myself sitting in front of the computer writing a textbook for my students. Writing a book is not something that you wake up and decide to do; it took me 10 years to decide to write a book after much prodding from former students and administrators. Then, it took me almost 2 years to write this book from start to finish. It was no easy feat.

This textbook combines the best of my knowledge with my own teachings. I created the **ABCDFG Method** to systematically guide the students in translating use cases and requirements to UML diagrams. I also introduce a new term called the **POWER Principles** that combine the "best" of the best software design principles out there. No other book that I know of systematically teaches and instructs step-by-step object-oriented analysis and design without having the student get lost in the sea of theory.

This textbook is for those with some prior programming experience. It is expected that the student has written some programs or want to know about how they can improve their software engineering through analysis and design. This textbook will not teach you to become an architect or guarantee you a job at a top software engineering company, but it will help you build a strong foundation in software engineering by teaching you how to think, how to use software principles, and most importantly, when to use them.

There are coding examples in this textbook using the JAVA and Python programming languages, which are currently two of the top 5 programming languages depending on who's conducting the research. Pseudo-code may also be used in my attempt to be program language agnostic.

Finally, I leave you, the reader, with one final remark before you set yourself free into this book: It's best to read in order and resist the temptation to skip around.

Enjoy it as much as I have enjoyed writing it.

/s/ Edwin

[This page left intentionally blank]

OOAD Cookbook:

Introduction to Practical System Modeling

[This page left intentionally blank]

1 OVERVIEW OF SOFTWARE ENGINEERING

1.1 Introduction

It's true: Designing *great* software is an art and a science. For me, the most enjoyable part of designing software is the ability to deliver a solution to a defined problem. I find that deeply satisfying. It might be because of my upbringing where puzzles and games were a large part of my childhood, but I've always wanted to solve problems.

As I learned about the "Scientific Process" in grade school and applied how to create hypotheses to tease out a possible solution, I learned that it was all a game – a game where you can tweak your strategy to deliver the desired results (not that I did this, but saw others that did). So naturally, I applied the Scientific Process to almost everything in my childhood, from playing board games, puzzles, to figuring people out. As I became more experienced, I realized that if the puzzles and games were all mechanical, it would be boring to solve and ripe for a machine to complete. But the art of it, the art of applying different methodologies, the art of

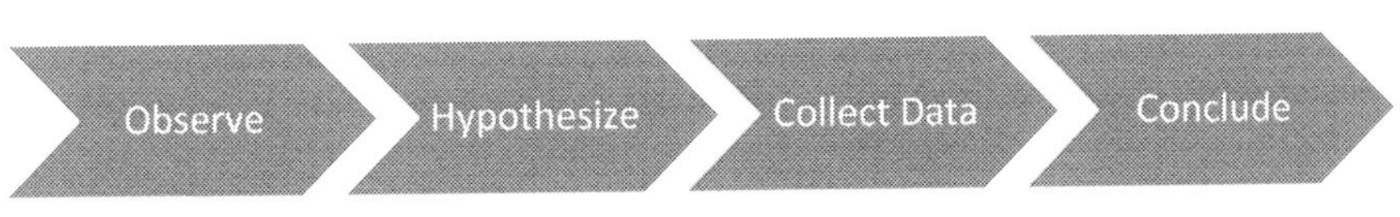

Simplified Scientific Process Diagram

communication, the art of working as a team, can't be replicated. It is what makes us human. It is what makes it fun.

When we design software, we also apply the Scientific Process, but for some reason, we don't call it that. Perhaps we've simply "outgrown" that term and we moved on to fancier words. Instead, we use terms like "Software Development Process" or "Object Oriented Design" among many others that you may already be familiar with. Using fancier terms does not necessarily change the process entirely, but over the past 40+ years of software design, software professionals have built upon the Scientific Process and designed very specific ways to solve software design problems, which warrant the use of new names.

Just like how science has evolved into collaborating with teams all over the world, designing software has also been upgraded from a person sitting in front of a giant machine to throngs of connected developers who can send code to each other at the speed of light. So, we rarely design in isolation. We do not lock ourselves up in the attic and appear downstairs 10 years later[1] to have solved all of humanity's computing problems. No. We work in teams. We communicate and miscommunicate. We understand and be misunderstood. We have fun as a team to solve a single common tangible goal and we make sure we deliver great software not only for the company that we work for, but for us, because our work defines us as engineers.

Role of OOAD in the Modern Era

Object Oriented Analysis and Design is one of the first courses a computer science/software engineering student learns after they have learned a programming language or two, data structures, and algorithms. Although a prerequisite in most computer science programs at top universities, data structures and algorithms are not prerequisites in understanding the materials in this book.

OOAD, for short, is what students use to apply the theory of what they learn to designing maintainable and modular software.

[1] Reference to Fermat's Last Theorem.

For some, the concepts laid out may be obvious – "Yea, how else would you do this if it were not object oriented?" a student might ask. In fact, there are many programming and design paradigms. Ever since the first machines designed by Alan Turing, programmers have had to express code on physical punch cards or tape. Fast forward almost a century later and we are expressing software on specialized programming environments such as Eclipse, Emacs, or vim, with the powers to auto generate parts of your software model. Programming has immensely changed over time for the better – for the software engineer. However, the problems that we need to solve are harder and more complex. While in the early 1900s, you may be asked to write software to break a 4-digit security code (you can enumerate all 10,000 possible combinations), the problems nowadays are how do we personalize medicine given the petabytes of data and genomes that may or may not be relevant.

This brings us back to OOAD and the work environment. You most likely will not be developing software for just yourself, and even if you did, you want to be able to **maintain** it (have you written some code 2 years ago and when you looked back you asked yourself 'what was I thinking?'), and minimize the number of lines of code that you write (why write more than what is needed? Why fix something that is not broken? Why recreate the wheel?). After all, software engineers are famous for being "lazy" due to their lack of wanting to rewrite code when a solution already exists, but in reality, we are just misunderstood for being "efficient".

Solving the problems of the future will require building systems that are easy to maintain and can be reused.

But let's not mistaken "efficiency" for doing the "minimum amount of work" at work just to get by. For some developers, "doing the minimum" is sufficient for their daily job. But if you want to do extremely well, you will need a solid foundation in problem solving and engineering principles to differentiate yourself among many other developers. In my experience, I have found that being able to solve problems concisely and the ability to convey it to others are what separates a good engineer versus a great engineer. I am sure all of you want to fall into the "great" engineer category.

Thus, this book will attempt to impart both the art and science of software engineering in the analysis and design process, by giving you as many examples as possible with responses that we will discuss, dissect, and learn from. It's a tall order, but I've been doing this for over a decade in class.

Yes, you will learn by first learning the theory, applying theories to the exercises in a step-by-step manner, and discussing various other potential solutions. After all, if you only learn from good examples, you will not be able to appreciate the elegance of the good solution. We will learn this material through the lens of "Object Oriented Analysis & Design" or what I refer to throughout the book as OOAD. This is a different technique that parallels the types of interview questions that are currently popular in software engineering interviews. Some examples that come to mind are: Design software for the elevator in your building, Design a remote control to dispense candy from the wall, or Design a phone application for the deaf.

We have tools to help us. Software engineers and developers need tools to solve a problem once they have identified what problem to solve. The tools come in many forms and complexities. We will be learning them: UML (or Unified Modeling language) to communicate our designs, design principles to help us come up with a solid design, and general problem-solving abilities to help you solve for a problem and not develop a solution to fit a problem.

The tools only help you to formulate and communicate your ideas.

This book focuses on those sets of tools as well as provides real world examples to show how what you learn fits in the overall scheme of things. Design patterns, which is a more advanced topic, is not all covered in this book; but some elementary concepts of design patterns will be discussed. If the reader wants a more advanced survey after completing this book, the reader is advised to research the "Gang of Four" for the 23 classic software Design Patterns.

In summary, this book covers the following topics: Software Engineering, Use Case and Requirements analysis, Writing a Design Specification, various forms of UML, OOAD Principles and best practices, and a short chapter on Agile and its relationship to OOAD.

1.2 The Big Picture

Are you catching a moving train?

Before we dive into OOAD, it is critical that we understand the overall software development process and see where OOAD fits in. Without this understanding, we are left solving bits and pieces without any connection to the overall process. When you start a new software job, for example, in some cases, you will start when the train is already running or you may be the person who will conduct the train. In either case, you will want to know what phase of the software development lifecycle (SDLC) you are in and you will want to know all the steps and process to get to where you want to go (i.e. end goal is most certainly releasing the product!).

Sometimes, no matter how experienced you may be, you will find yourself "lost" in SDLC. From time to time, you will ask yourself, "What are we really solving for? What am I asked to do? What's my role?" and that is perfectly acceptable especially in environments that may lack a lot of process. And even on teams that have all the processes in place, you may ask yourself, "Are these the right ones that we should follow?"

Are you building a new train?

Even so, continuing to ask yourself those questions help give you clarity in what functions and roles you may help your team to serve. It may be the case that your role will change from time to time where you may be coding in a sprint (an Agile terminology, which we will cover later) and pushing buttons to deploy code in the cloud in the next. So, having that sense of awareness of your role and the flexibility of which you may approach your work will help you be a better software engineer.

The Software Development process is different for different companies and even within companies

You should also know that the SDLC depends very much on your specific company and/or team. Each team may have different development environments and culture, and teams even within the same company may operate differently than other teams. As we will discuss the various types of SDLC in the next chapter, we end this section knowing that processes could be different from company to company and team to team, which will dictate how you work and what you do as a software engineer.

But fear not, while the SDLC may change from team to team or from company to company, OOAD does not. OOAD is a software engineering methodology that is independent of any SDLC. Books and resources that try to tie OOAD to agile development miss the foundation of what OOAD is all about – Given a problem, how to analyze and how to design software that is independent of other extraneities.

Let me summarize what you have read so far:

- Object Oriented Analysis and Design (OOAD) is foundational in what we do as software engineers.
- There is both art and science in the OOAD process, and this book tries to codify the art aspects.
- UML is the common design language that software engineers use to convey their designs.

1.3 The SDLC Process – A High Level Overview

If you are currently working in an engineering role (i.e. software engineer, quality engineer, devops engineer), you know the SDLC process of your company. (If you are currently a student, fear not, this section tells you how it's done). This process is codified into a set of rules that guide what engineers must do to ship code to their customers. You break any part of the rules and you are probably not going to ship code that day. Larger companies have a more rigid set of rules because large companies must follow standards either imposed on them by government compliance standards, customer expectations, or by themselves.

A quote I often hear is, "This is the way [i.e. SDLC process] that we have always done things" or "We don't do it that way" in the context of software development leaves opportunities for others to "do it the other way" and often the most efficient way.

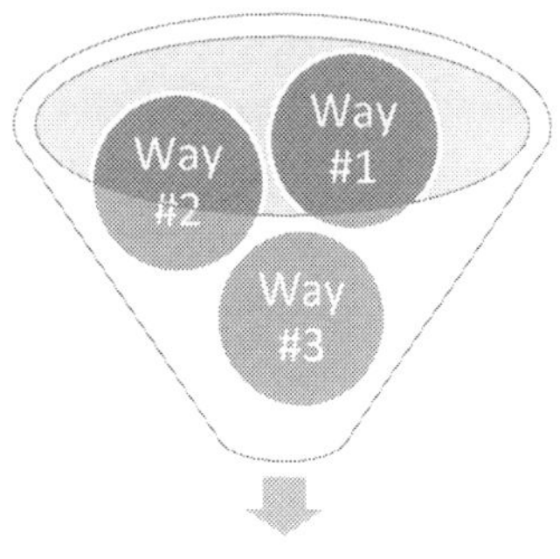

Start-up software development process

Larger corporation software development process

On the other hand, smaller companies are one example where they "do it the other way". They don't necessarily have to follow the rules and regulations because it may be too prohibitive to do so. They need to make money quick by shipping their product or the whole company may not survive. This kind of "move fast" mentality makes sense when you are small and nimble, but when you are a much larger company, moving fast may break things that may cause detrimental harm to the company.

If you are a student and haven't worked in a company in an engineering capacity, you probably have no idea what the last few paragraphs were referencing, and that's okay. Because what I'm going to tell you next means that not all of it matters in the context of OOAD.

OOAD is independent of company size. Larger companies benefit more from OOAD.

Yes, the SDLC may be different on a company size perspective (as we've established), but the underlying foundation of determining what the problem is through analysis and then designing is the same no matter where you are.

In fact, there is a striking similarity to where most SDLC processes come from and the various branches that are originating from it. My hypothesis is that it originated from OOAD.

OOAD is independent of company size.

As we mentioned in the last section, processes could be radically different. Think back – you were writing code, you tested it, you wrote some documentation, you deployed the software, and your day was done.

Let's structure this a bit more.

In Figure 1.1, we see a high-level overview of the SDLC process. It starts with the requirements and use cases phase. In this phase, the software engineer must understand the use cases and requirements that is written

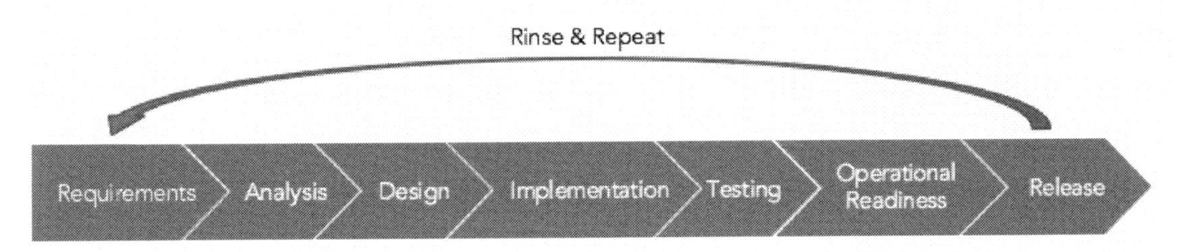

Figure 1.1

usually by a Product Manager, Product Owner, or Marketing person[2]. In chapter 3, we discuss how to write use cases so that as an engineer, you are able to understand them and appreciate the work that goes into them. Furthermore, you may be required to come up with technical use cases as well in your Analysis and Design phase to describe technical aspects of your design such as interaction between different parts of the system where the user, for example, might be a service calling another service.

After the **Requirements** phase comes the **Analysis** Phase. In this phase, the engineer may ask clarifying questions or even come up with internal use cases at a more technical level than what the PM first proposed.

In a nutshell, the Analysis phase is understanding, discovering, and investigating the problem and its use cases and then refining the requirements. This back-and-forth between engineering and PM constitute the Analysis phase. This is when the engineers fully understand the use cases and requirements and takes that as input to the next phase, which is the Design phase. Before we move on to the Design phase, I want to make clear that although the diagram shows the arrow going from Requirements to Analysis, in reality is a double ended arrow (the "back-and-forth" that I mentioned earlier between PM and engineering). This is an important observation since we as engineers should understand where the requirements come from.

... The **Analysis** phase is understanding, discovering, and investigating the problem ...

In the **Design** phase, engineers come up with a conceptual model of the solution. This is where Unified Modeling Language (UML) is one communication artifact to convey the design of what you are building. Other artifacts could be written documentation, structured or unstructured diagrams, relationship diagrams, etc. Regardless of whatever diagram you choose to use, the general concept is to (1) represent the system, (2) show how each important part of the system interacts with each other, (3) show what each parts of the system are and do, and (4) show how each parts are inter-related. Although UML is one communication tool, it is a very

... The **Design** phase is coming up with the conceptual model of the solution ...

[2] Terms and titles may vary from company to company. But the general gist is that there is a person usually dedicated to communicating what to build. In this book, we will refer to this person as the "PM".

important communication tool. In this book, we will cover UML to represent many types of diagrams that are important communication and design tools.

After the Design phase comes the **Implementation phase**. In this phase, design becomes reality in the form of functioning code. One or more programming languages are used to translate the design into code. This is where we as software engineers "churn out code"[3]. The software code is then packaged up into a library, an executable, or web service.

When the implementation phase is complete, the **testing phase** starts. This phase usually means that a separate team takes the software package and tests it for bugs, errors, corner cases – basically if the code is performing to specification. Bugs that are reported get sent back to the developer for fixing. (Actually, this is too simplistic. In the real world, not every bug is fixed. In fact, bugs are prioritized and only the ones deemed most important are fixed.)

There are two things I'd like to mention:

(1) The developer has most likely tested his code before the code hits the testing phase. She has most likely written some unit tests and ran tests against those. Her team has also probably automated a bunch of tests so that every time she checks in code, a job to kick off the testing process begins. The automated testing may take hours depending on the complexity of the code base and tests. If any code fails (as in a "breaking change", the check-in is aborted and the change must be rolled back, which means to revert back to the codebase without the newly checked-in code. Anyway, so it's not like the developer didn't test any of her code before it hits the testing phase.

(2) Recall earlier that I said "usually means a separate team", which is not always the case. A lot of the quality assurance testing is being automated for reasons that this book will not go into. So instead of dealing with a separate "QA" team, your code may go through only automated testing before some customers see it.

Operational readiness is the phase that starts after testing, assuming all tests that need to pass are passed. Operational readiness is the testing of the code to absorb issues in deploying, scaling, and use for customers.

SIDE BAR

Readers may realize that in current devops models (where the developer plays both roles as developer and operations), the devops engineers is in charge of writing the code, testing it, and deploying it. Conflicts of interests aside (because the developer is less inclined to find bugs in his code), this model is becoming more popular at cloud-based companies that offer Software-As-A-Service (SaaS).

[3] "Churn out code" is an industry terminology to represent one part of what software engineers do. Sadly, most people think that's the only part we do and what they don't understand is that software engineers spend more of their time analyzing and designing than actually writing code. Either way, just like in the 1800s where households churned butter, in 2000s software engineers churn code.

Operational readiness is mainly used for web applications or cloud services, where more and more companies are moving their software to the cloud (and most likely charging a recurring revenue model or offering it for free in return of advertisement placement). Software that is embedded in chips, for example, usually do not go through operational readiness stages, but instead go through more stringent testing and various edge cases. After all, once hardware ships, it is near impossible to get it back aside from the costs of a recall; you want to make sure you have zero bugs. As a case study, use your favorite search engine for "Intel Pentium bug", where the premier processor company found bugs after shipping. Intel has experienced issues with their chips after shipment not once, but several times in their history. Fortunately, some bugs can be fixed with a firmware update.

Another example is medical devices. If there is a bug in how it detects your heart rate, for example, you could be falsely diagnosed with a medical condition or not diagnosed when you truly have the condition. While this particular example is more relevant in the testing phase, operational readiness is the packaging it up for consumer use so sometimes I will use these two terms to mean that bugs and issues should be detected in one or both of the phases.

Software in the cloud, on the other hand, don't generally face the same scrutiny unless for mission critical applications. If Google decides to ship you a new feature for Gmail, the web-based email program, and the new feature has a bug, regardless of what it is (in most cases), Google can quickly fix the bug in the backend almost immediately without having to do any recalls or customer outreach. This is a paradigm shift in software engineering where software can be shipped at any time – and fixed at any time. This was different in the 1980s and 1990s where software was bought literally off the shelf at computer stores just like you would go into a convenience store to buy a box of cereal. Again, if bugs in the software were found, it was difficult to get the software back and provide patches or updates to the software in the absence of the Internet.

Lastly, when the software has gone through readiness and various levels of testing, it will be released. Actually, it may be the case in the cloud services model, where software is released as a service, that software is not fully tested. Sure, there are regression tests that are run on a daily basis, but new software sometimes depend on the actual users to find any bugs. If any bugs are found, then the devops engineer can quickly roll back any changes. This model is the CICD or Continuous Integration and Continuous Delivery model, where software, as the acronym implies, is always being integrated into production code and always available to the customer right after its written by the engineer.

CICD is popular among cloud-based software companies.

I have just explained at a high level a typical software development lifecycle for almost all software development projects. Any variations of this, such as terms you may have heard or have experience with "agile", "waterfall", "scrum" all originate from this lifecycle but vary it in a way that works best for the type of software project, the company, and the team.

We will examine various other software development practices in a future chapter of this book.

We are at the end of the SDLC – or are we? One more step, which is the feedback loop from when the customer experiences with the newly released software to the feedback the customer provides to improve the product. The cycle repeats again until after every iteration, the software gets less bug free, more features, and faster.

The [SDLC] cycle repeats again until after every iteration, the software gets less bug free, more features, and faster.

Regardless of what SDLC process you use, the general diagram above holds true in almost all cases. There are caveats to this, but I have not seen this work successfully every time in practice, but I may have limited exposure. One example is this: there are some teams that code first, determine the problem later; this is the classic build it and they will come model. This model is high risk as you do not yet have customers lined up to use what you are building and instead hoping that you will find them or problems that it solves when you are done. It's counterintuitive, but has worked for successful companies.

Some believe that the "build it and they will come" model is really a fallacy. Apple Inc., one of the most successful companies of all time, claims that they do not do marketing and so they have an innate ability to determine what their customers want without their customers knowing what they want. And so, the story goes, Apple goes and builds fantastic products such as the iPod or the iPhone to wild successes without asking a single customer tell them what they want out of a music player or phone; Apple knows best. Some may argue further and say, "well, if you ask the customer in the 1900s if they wanted a car, they would have preferred a faster horse and buggy." All fair statements. Truth is, Apple does do research, and you probably wouldn't ask people who are accustomed to something whether they want to try something radically new and unfamiliar. Because almost always the customer would say "no".

Now that you have a good sense of the SDLC process, in the next chapter, we can turn our attention to one part of the SDLC process: Requirements and Analysis. But before we get there, a little history lesson on programming paradigms.

1.4 Overview of Programming Paradigms

When we discuss Object Oriented Programming (OOP) or Object-Oriented Design (OOD)[4], it's also important for us to understand where the idea came from. As we discussed before, OOP/OOD is a programming and design methodology; it is one way to go about solving problems in software engineering via **code organization, programming language selection, and code execution**.

[4] OOP and OOD will be used interchangeably throughout this textbook.

Many ways exists so this section will provide an overview of the various programming paradigms and see where OOP/OOD fit in. There are over a dozen types of programming paradigms ranging from concurrent programming to action programming to declarative programming to many, many others. While this section will not do justice to all the different types, we will focus at a high level the important and most commonly used paradigms.

OO is one way to go about solving problems in software engineering via **code organization, programming language selection, and code execution**

1.4.1 Imperative Programming

Imperative programming is a programming paradigm that focuses on the expression of commands to execute a defined sequence of code. As a programmer, we write lines of code or statements that tell the computer exactly what to do and when to do it; this is imperative programming. This is the most common form of programming and the way that we first learned how to program on the computer. When we first learned how to program, we picked up a book (such as "How to program in JAVA" or "Introduction to Python" or something similar) that walked us through what to type in front of our computers so we can instruct the computer exactly what to do.

```
// we wrote code like this

a = 5
b = 6
c = a + b
print c
```

In the example, we first instructed the computer to assign 5 to a variable "a". Next, we told the computer to assign 6 to "b". Then we added "a" and "b" together to get "c". Finally, we asked the computer to print the value of "c", which it does. There is an ordering, a sequence, and each statement is a specific instruction that the computer must follow in that specific order. We call this imperative programming and it should already be familiar to you.

Programming languages such as JAVA, Python, C, C++, C#, and many, many others are all imperative programming languages. Algorithms can be more easily programmed in imperative languages because it gives the programmer a sense of order and control over how things should happen. All the aforementioned programming languages are object-oriented programming languages (but they don't have to be programmed in an object-oriented way!)

1.4.2 Declarative Programming

Declarative programming is a programming paradigm that focuses on the logic of the code rather than the sequence of code execution. This is the exact opposite of imperative programming. This means that when an algorithm is written in declarative programming, the sequence of the code execution becomes the responsibility of the programming language, not the programmer. This is in direct contrast to imperative programming, which is focused on the code execution and telling the computer how to do it, rather than telling the computer what needs to be done.

```
// Declarative example

<HTML>
 <HEAD>
  <TITLE>This is a title</TITLE>
 </HEAD>
 <BODY>Hi, this is Declarative</BODY>
</HTML>
```

In the HTML example, we didn't tell the computer exactly what to do. The computer doesn't have to read the code top down or in any order. We only told the computer to display whatever it is I want displayed, but the code never specified how to do it. The interpreter of the HTML (i.e. a web browser) will render the HTML and process it to display it accordingly. It may decide to process the body first, before it processes the head tags; either way, there is no ordering, just that whatever I want displayed, it will display it. Another way to think about it is "I want the end result, and I don't care how it's done".

Some languages that exhibit this behavior are SQL and HTML, none of which is an object-oriented programming language.

1.4.3 Structured Programming

Structured programming is a programming paradigm that focuses on how the code is structured with the ultimate goal of making the code easy to maintain and easy to read, thereby reducing development time. If code is arranged in blocks, then code that is together is logically segregated from one another. Structured programming achieves this by allowing the programmer to define these logical blocks via "if,then,else" statements, loops, subroutines, or blocks (such as BEGIN… END).

Structured programming is almost synonymous with procedural programming, which is most likely the way that we first learned how to program – whereby we learned how to section off pieces of code that do certain tasks but we ultimately ended up having a super long file with all our code in it.

```
// this next block of code will determine whether I need to buy
a new car or not

if salary > 100000:
   print "Yes, new car time!"
elsif salary > 50000:
   print "Just a few more months…"
else:
   print "Can't buy a new car now.. sorry!"
```

Some languages that exhibit this behavior are C, Pascal, COBOL, PL/I, and others. Suffice to say, these programming languages are not very popular anymore, but is still heavily used in certain types of software environments.

Structured programming gave way to more advanced programming methodologies such as object oriented. Object oriented borrowed the block concepts and extended it to modules/classes.

1.4.4 Functional Programming

Functional programming has its origins in mathematic formulas. What's neat about it is that is a form of declarative programming in that, although the programmer states the formula, the computer decides how to best execute it. And unlike imperative programming, functional programming does not change state.

Some languages that exhibit this behavior are SQL, Lisp, Scheme, and R (statistics).

```
// Scheme example

(define (map (lambda (x y) (+ x y)))
```

We've defined a function called "map" that takes in 2 parameters, which adds them together. Map is the name of the lambda function. By using functions, instead of shared state, functional programming emphasizes expressions rather than the execution of statements as it exists in non-functional programming paradigms. The example below provides an example of a "non-functional" programming, where state is used instead of derived functions.

```
// Non-functional programming example

x = 5
y = 2

z = x+y
```

1.4.5 Natural Language Programming

Although not object oriented related, programming with boxes or programming with any spoken human language will become more popular. Imagine if we could instruct a computer to do something just be speaking the same languages that humans communicate. We have this today with the many voice assistant programs in Apple's Siri, Google's Assistant, and Amazon's Alexa. But they are really good at doing single tasks and not long programs.

```
Me: Siri, make an appointment with Tom at 5PM
tomorrow at the cafeteria for some coffee.

Siri: [processing..]

Siri: I have made an appointment at 5PM.
```

What if we could write longer programs in written English? This somewhat exists today. You have a special interpreter who understands the natural language either as spoken or written, and then behind the scenes converts that into a computer language like Python to execute. There are some that are able to do this today but are mostly reserved for specialized tasks. Wolfram Alpha, one of the most advanced mathematical and science programs today, is an example of this.

Why is this important? Natural language programming is currently reserved for simple or single tasks. But there will be a day where it will be able to tackle more complicated programs. How would this change or alter object-oriented programming? Will the system automatically convert the commands to OO? Will we need to maintain any code at all if the system will do it? Hmm.. Food for thought.

1.5 Examples of Object-Oriented Languages

You have most likely encountered an Object-Oriented programming language. It was most likely one of the first languages you learned to program (unless your first language was Scheme or Lisp). So, you most likely already have an idea of what an OO language is. But in case you do not, here are some examples of OO languages, but remember, you can use any of the languages in non-object-oriented ways, because OO is a methodology and the programmer must enforce this, not the program or the system.

Another nuance is that some programming languages belong to one or more of programming paradigms. So, a programming language could be both procedural and object oriented. Furthermore, a programming language could have object-oriented features, but not be totally object oriented.

In the table below are selected programming languages out of many, many programming languages out there that are noteworthy object-oriented programming languages or languages that exhibit object-oriented features.

Programming Language	Is it Object Oriented?
C++	C++ is considered to have object-oriented features, because its origin is in the C programming language. The name C++ means "C with classes".
C#	Created by Microsoft, C# is a multi-paradigm programming language that is considered to be imperative, declarative, object oriented, among other programming language paradigms.
Go	Created by Google, Go (or Golang), which is more suitable for parallel programming/processing, is also a multi-paradigm programming language that can be object oriented as well.
Java	Created by Sun Microsystems, Java is a multi-paradigm programming language but its roots are in object oriented .
MATLAB	MATLAB, a proprietary programming language that is mainly used for science and math applications, supports object-oriented features such as classes and inheritance.
Objective-C	Objective-C, mainly for Apple's mobile applications, is a multi-paradigm and object-oriented programming language.
Perl	Perl has long been a scripting language, but since Perl v5, has built in support for object-oriented features. Perl is considered to be a multi-paradigm programming language – supporting object oriented, functional, and imperative paradigms.
Python	Similar to Perl, Python is a multi-paradigm programming language and supports object oriented, functional, and imperative paradigms.
Ruby	Ruby is a multi-paradigm programming language and support object-oriented paradigm.
Scala	Scala, similar to Java, is a multi-paradigm programming language with its roots in functional programming but supports object-oriented paradigm.

1.6 Learning OOAD Too Late

Good software engineers finish the job, but when they want to add new features to an existing system, modify a component so it does x instead of y, or even remove a feature, it will take time because the software that they built may not necessarily be flexible; it's not modular enough that they could just delete the code to remove the feature, but the code in question also inter-relates with other codes that affect other features. This coupling of code slows down progress.

You may argue that the job of the engineer is complete after they complete all the requirements! No one would argue with that! But the long answer is that it's much more nuanced than that. We engineers are never done. There will always be bugs and feature requests. There will always be opportunities to make our code run faster or perform better. But we don't always think ahead because we are too focused on getting code out the door.

Let me tell you a story.

I once wrote software in non-object-oriented ways (Gasp!). My job was to write an automatic blog software system. It was my personal project back in the day before blogs were popular. This was pre-dot-com bubble. This was like LiveJournal except that I never made any money off of my work.

My methodology as a young engineer with some free time was to think of what I needed this system to do since I was both the developer and the primary user. I wanted it so that when I wrote a blog entry, it would be through a dynamic HTML interface, instead of writing my blog post in SQL and manually inserting into a database. I wanted it so that readers can get an RSS feed. I wanted a slick DHTML interface with JavaScript. (You may need to do some googling of terms that I am throwing out here such as RSS and SQL and HTML). I wanted things easier for me so that the less that I interact with the system code the better.

Well, it turns out I "finished" designing this system in a few months. My life was content… until one of my readers (friend) asked me how they can comment on my blog posts.

Great feature request, I replied! Too bad that it took me a lot of time to refactor my code to make commenting on a per blog entry basis work. If I had used the object-oriented way, my life would have been much easier because I would write less new code and refactor less existing code.

The lesson is clear. Things will change. Your design is good, but it's only good for those requirements that were initially specified. When someone adds or removes something, it tests how durable (or fragile) your design is. Great design means that your system is able to accommodate additions, deletions, and modifications with ease. It doesn't mean that they will be "free" in time or money or development effort; it means that it's easier to make the change.

1.7 Where does Design Patterns or Principles fit?

Logically, we first need to get a basic foundation in order to discuss Design Principles. Once you have "mastered" the Design Principles, then you can move on to study Design Patterns, which is not part of this book.

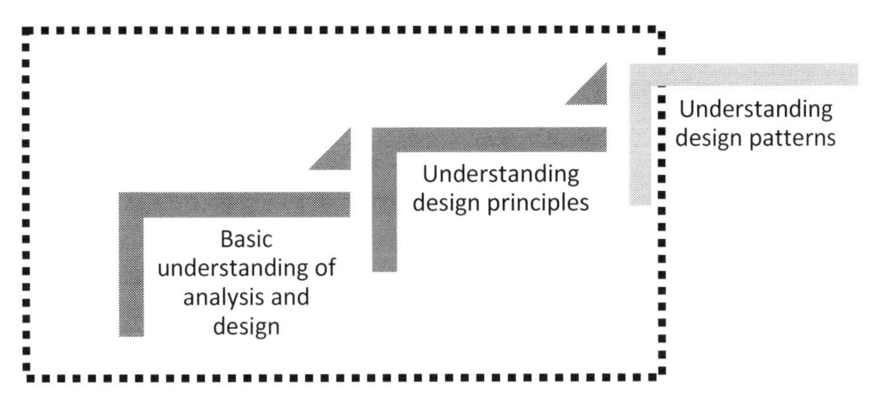

In the next few chapters, you will gain a thorough understanding of the underlying foundation in object-oriented analysis and design. We will examine the use case, requirements, and how to translate them into artifacts. **Once we are comfortable, we will move forward to design principles to help refine those artifacts**.

Design Principles are software design principles used to determine responsibilities of classes and objects and how they should or should not interact with each other. There are many, many design principles such as GRASP, SOLID, KISS, DRY, and others. Studying them all is one way to tackle this subject. However, I think there may be a more efficient way by studying the most important concepts and principles and use generalization and abstraction methodologies to help gain both breadth and depth.

In this book, I introduce, a combination of software design principles amalgamed into a set of succinct and straightforward principles called the **POWER Principles**.

The POWER Principles, which you will learn in the subsequent chapters, is like all the best and most relevant principles attended a Board of Directors meeting (an important meeting) and said, "Ok, let's simplify all these principles in a way that any software engineer can understand but still be useful to both advanced and introductory students". So, the POWER Principles were born!

Once you have a powerful grasp of design principles, you will want to study the Design Patterns, which are pre-made solutions to common software problems. This book doesn't cover Design Patterns and recommend that the reader study the Gang of Four Design Patterns, which are the de-facto standard.

Now, onwards to Analysis!

[This page left intentionally blank]

1.8 Chapter Review Questions

1. What software development process are you already familiar with? It could be a previous company or ones you have read about.
2. What is important about the software development process?
3. What is Object Oriented Analysis and Design?
4. What do you do in the Analysis phase?
5. What do you do in the Design phase?
6. Which artifacts in the analysis or design phase can be implemented?
7. When was the last time you wrote code, then came back to it a few years later, but couldn't understand it anymore? What would you do to help resolve this?
8. Name 3 object-oriented programming languages.
9. When should you learn Design Patterns?

[This page left intentionally blank]

2 Analysis: Requirements & Use Cases

While software engineers almost never write requirements and use cases, they must understand them and be able to translate the collection of requirements for a specific problem into a solution that solves the problem. In this chapter, we will learn to understand, write, and look at examples of requirements. We will use the requirements as the basis for the examples used throughout this book. And to be clear, this book does not explain how to gather requirements or learn where they come from (as it should not); instead, this book assumes that someone has written the requirements and it is our job to understand, discuss, and/or tell whoever wrote it that either the requirements are feasible or infeasible.

2.1 Requirements versus Use Cases

Some may confuse the difference between requirements and use cases in the real world and in some cases, those words are used interchangeable. However, in this textbook, and most work environments, it is critical that we differentiate between the two.

A requirements is a "condition or capability" that a user or system needs to "achieve an objective".

Requirement Example: The ice cream machine must allow the user to press a button to dispense a single scoop of ice cream.

The official definition is in the IEEE Standard Glossary of Software Engineering Terminology, but the definition above suffices in all cases. The origin of the word **requirement**, I believe, comes from the need or "requirement" for the software or system to do "something". In fact, some people refer to requirements as "needs" as well. So, hearing "I don't fully understand what the customer *needs*" or "Those *needs* are ambiguous, we need him to define the *needs* more clearly" can be heard in software company hallways. In fact, hearing those statements often, I would argue, is a good thing as it helps the team converge on what problem we are truly solving for. When we understand the needs, we understand the requirements of what we need to build. In the ice cream machine example, we are requiring that whatever ice cream machine that engineering builds, it *has to* have a button and that button when pressed outputs a single scoop of ice cream. This requirement, actually, has many open questions: "What does the button look like? What flavors of ice cream does it dispense? What happens when no ice cream comes out? What does this ice cream machine look like? How big is it?" Those open questions are a great segue into "use case".

> *A use case is a set of steps that define from a user or system perspective what needs to happen to achieve an objective.*

Use Case Example: At the request of the customer who wants strawberry ice cream, the ice cream machine operator presses a series of buttons to dispense strawberry ice cream. First, the operator selects "strawberry" flavor from the touch screen panel. Then, she pushes the button marked "dispense" on the machine. The operator puts a sugar cone underneath where the scoop of ice cream will come out. A few moments later, the scoop of strawberry ice cream falls onto the cone. The operator takes the cone out and presents it to the customer.

Notice the difference. A requirement is usually one condition; it is best that a requirement be measurable. But, a use case can be one or more conditions. In fact, use cases can be broken down into software requirements; a requirement usually cannot be broken down into a use case as it is unidirectional.

Notice the similarities. Both are written in text (not a diagram – although diagrams are perfectly acceptable but it is important that the text be written first) and accomplish an objective or goal. Can you see in what part of the use case the original requirement came from? Can our requirement be written better? You bet. Requirements should be measurable and be exact as possible, without going into detail about *how* the internal workings of the system works. Requirements define the *what*, not the how. Use cases express the flow of how a user uses the system or service you are building, but does not explain how the system internally works. We don't talk about how the machine has to connect to the internet and ice cream flavors database or the exact software code that needs to be written; those are too low-level detail and are not from a user perspective. Users do not care what happens internally, all they care about are what they see, what they want, and what they get; writing a use case is basically treating the system as a black box where you only know the inputs and outputs.

Let's review:

Use Case characteristics	Requirement characteristics
• Text • Story (logical ordering from start to finish) • Shows how the user accomplishes a goal	• Text • Measurable • Derived from use case(s)

The requirements are written in text and almost never in any other form (not a drawing, not a picture); just plain text. The text itself must be readable, clear, and concise. In fact, the term we use here is called "measurable", meaning that it is able to be satisfied as a whole. So, if a requirement is actually a collection of requirements, then what if some requirements are not satisfied? This means the entire requirement collection is not satisfied, making it difficult to track. Therefore, it's best that each requirement is its own atomic requirement: A ball should be yellow; not a ball should be yellow and 12" in diameter - which would be two requirements. There are lots more to know about use cases and requirements. Before we dive deeper into the different types and components of use cases and requirements, we take a slight detour into a document that all engineers should familiarize themselves with: the PRD.

Use Case versus Requirement
Do you know the differences?

2.2 The Products Requirements Document (PRD)

Let's take a step back. Where do these use cases and requirements even come from? (And why do we have to follow it?). What if I don't believe the use case is feasible? What if the use case doesn't make sense?

You're asking the right questions and this is the perfect time to research more deeply so that in the future chapters, we take what is written as use cases and requirements and turn them into a solution.

The PRD defines the product – what the engineering team should build and why

The PRD or Products Requirement Document is a document usually written by the Product Manager, Product Owner, or Pro duct Marketing Manager. In some companies, it's written by a Program Manager (Microsoft). Some product managers are technical, some are not; you can usually tell if they are or not by either speaking with them or seeing one of their deliverables, which is the PRD. The PRD defines the product – what the engineering team is building and why. The PRD doesn't tell how the product is be built, that's the engineers job. The PRD, if written correctly and properly, can be taken by engineers and turned into *a design of* a working solution. So, it's critical that we understand what's usually in a PRD (varies by companies), but some sections never change.

2.2.1 Sections of a PRD

We will briefly examine the two main sections of the PRD: The Why and the What.

The Why. This part of the PRD attempts to explain why the company should build this. Based on market analysis, user studies, customer feedback and any combinations thereof, the author distills all the data into an imaginary product – a product with a vision that satisfies certain company objectives such as revenue or market share. This section is important for engineers to understand as it provides context into what we wish to build. Can you imagine building a product and not knowing why it needs to be built? Now you know where to find out why: the PRD.

After reading this section, you as an engineer must be convinced that this is the product to build. Because if you are not convinced, then you are uncertain "why" you should be building this.

The What. The "What" explains Use Cases that this solution will address and subsequently the Requirements derived from the Use Cases. This section should be crystal clear to you and you should be able to take this document and start designing the solution that addresses the use cases and the requirements.

2.2.2 The What - Use Cases

Use cases answer the WHAT, not the HOW.

The PRD usually lists use cases in prioritized order from highest priority to lowest in hopes that the highest priority ones get completed before the lowest priority ones. Actually, the correct way to read this is that the author really wants everything completed (or else why would she write it?) but realizes that deep down, the MVP (or minimally viable product) doesn't need them all. The thinking is that if there's "extra" time, then the low priority asks will get completed.

The type of use cases in a PRD is similar to the ice cream machine example above. This type of use case is called a "brief use case". Brief use cases are about a paragraph long. We discuss the 3 types of use cases in the next section.

Additionally, not only does the PRD document the use cases for the positive scenarios, where the user successfully accomplishes the goal, but also negative scenarios where the user hits an error. Negative scenarios provide engineering a complete picture of the various possibilities while interacting with the system to make sure that each possibility is handled appropriately. Now of course, there are many possibilities and may be too many to enumerate. That's understandable. So, the best approach is to categorize each of the possible errors so that you enumerate the categories and types of errors instead of enumerating every possible error workflow, which will be time consuming and possibly redundant or even understood (obvious) by the engineering team.

2.2.3 Requirements

The requirements exist if and only if there exists a use case, after all, requirements are derived from use cases. One use case will have 1 or more requirements. It is not uncommon to see a single use case have over 10+ requirements. Usually, each requirement is a single measurable condition; clumping or collecting all the requirements in one single requirement is difficult for tracking purposes. As an example, if engineers decide that they can build condition A but not condition B of requirement X, is the requirement satisfied? Not really. Thus, it is much better that each condition A and B, be separate requirements so that A or B or both can be marked satisfied.

Requirements work the same way as use cases – they should answer the WHAT, not HOW.

2.2.4 Putting it all together

Let's make everything concrete with an example. You are tasked with designing a new product that does not exist in the marketplace; it is entirely new. The requirements call for an ice cream machine. This machine will take as input various flavors, water, sugar and output a scoop of ice cream on your ice cream cone. This is a high-tech machine and quite an engineering feat to get this right. **You want to design the software system internals** that controls how the user interacts with the machine, how the machine operates, and finally the end state of the machine when the scoop of ice cream makes the soft drop on the ice cream cone.

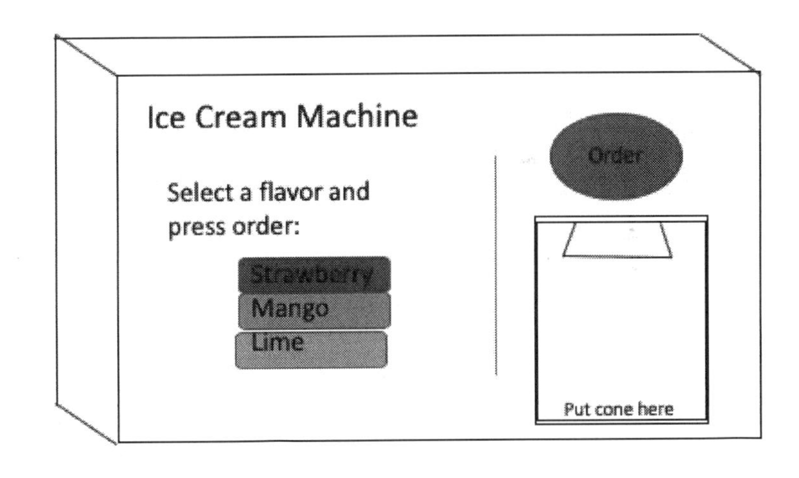

Here's what this machine looks like, at least, this is my "mockup" of what the machine looks like. A mockup is a pictorial diagram or drawing of what the product looks like. It doesn't have to be the look and feel of the "final" product; instead, it only shows our intentions of what the product that we wish to build looks like in our mind. So, for example, the mockup shows the ice cream machine as a rectangular box shape and looks kind of bulky. The real product that will ship to customers may or may not look like the drawing – the real product could ship with wheels or be a different color or be a different shape. Those details, which we call design details, are not covered in this textbook (as we want to focus on software design).

On the next page is an example of a PRD of this fictional product. You will almost never find complete and real PRDs of real products as those are company confidential and contains a lot of competitive information.

So, you'd probably only find templates of PRD's online. We'll show you the relevant sections of the PRD of our vision of the ice cream machine as mentioned above.

PRD Example:

Use Case ID/ Requirement ID	Description	Priority
UC-001	*Setup: The buyer of this ice cream machine would like to be able to set the machine on the table, plug it into a 120-volt outlet, turn it on with a flip of a switch that is easy to reach, and have the ice cream machine ready to use in 15 minutes so that he can start dispensing ice cream to his customers.*	High
REQ-001	The shape of the system must allow it to be placed on a flat table without tipping over.	High
REQ-002	The system must support a 120-volt power plug.	High
REQ-003	The on/off switch should be located in the front of the machine.	High
REQ-004	After the on switch is flipped, the machine must turn on.	High
REQ-005	The machine must be preloaded with ice cream making materials.	High
REQ-006	The machine must be ready to dispense ice cream in 15 minutes.	High
UC-002	*User order: At the request of the customer who wants strawberry ice cream, the ice cream machine operator presses the strawberry ice cream button first then presses "Order" button.. The operator then puts a sugar cone underneath where the scoop of ice cream will come out in 1 minute. A few moments later, the scoop of strawberry ice cream falls onto the cone. The operator takes the cone out and presents it to the customer.*	High
REQ-010	The system must have buttons for each flavor that is offered.	High
REQ-011	The system must have a "Strawberry" flavor button.	High
REQ-012	The system must have an "Order" button, which when pressed, orders the flavor that was most previously pressed.	High
REQ-013	The system must have space to place and hold the ice cream cone.	High
REQ-014	After the order button is pressed, the ice cream scoop must come out within a minute.	High
REQ-015	The scoop must fall onto the ice cream cone. The system must detect that there is an ice cream cone before dispensing the scoop of ice cream.	High
REQ-016	The order button must be painted red color.	Low

What did we just see? We saw two use cases (UC-001 and UC-002) with requirements underneath them. Those requirements were written to satisfy the referenced use case. In order to satisfy the use case, each and every one of those requirements must be satisfied. By satisfaction of the requirement, is it implemented and working just as described in the use case of the end user. If it is, then the requirement is satisfied. If it is not, either due to a bug or not implemented, then we say the requirement is not satisfied.

You will also see another column called "Priority". The priority is how important this requirement or use case is to the customer. If it's labelled "High" it usually means that this requirement is mandatory and that there isn't much room for negotiation. If it's marked "Low", then this is not an important requirement so it becomes a "good to have, but not significant" feature.

The contents of the use cases and requirements depict one product manager's perspective in how the use case and requirements are written. You can see that the requirements are mostly atomic – they are very specific and does not try to add too many items to a single requirement line item. You can also see that there is a clear mapping between the use cases and requirements; in some cases, a direct translation. However, as we will see later on, as an engineer, you will be looking at this document and trying to build what the product manager is envisioning. You should ask yourself, "Do you have all the information you need to start and finish building?" If the answer is "Yes", then the PRD was well-written, and that's good news. If the answer is "No", then the PRD is missing detail and so needs clarification or sometimes justification. Can you think of some details that are missing? As an example, here's one: how big is this table that we need to build the machine one? Is it like a small table? A counter top? Size is an important missing detail.

It's crucial that all engineers learn to read a PRD

A PRD can be a lengthy document, but it's crucial that all engineers learn to read this because this is where we get information about what to build. In fact, this is the only information that we as engineers have on what to build. We have to understand the use case and its corresponding requirements and possibly even ask questions about why some requirements may or may not be missing or ask clarifications. We may even come back to the author/product manager and say this requirement or use case is not technically feasible. Which ones do you think are "doable" and which ones do you think are outrageous?

We looked at really the main section of the PRD that mainly concerns us engineers. Other sections of a PRD that are not covered in this book and has little relevance are:

- Competitive Analysis
- Financial Projections
- And others

We say they have "little relevance" because it doesn't help us design better software. After all, those analysis in those sections should be reflected in the use cases and requirements anyway. For example, if competitor offers a "1-button ordering" system, then we may create use cases and requirements that will allow us to either match that 1-button ordering system or do away with buttons! The Product Manager, in most cases, should define what to build and why so that the engineers can take the requirements, understand them, and build to that vision.

2.3 Use Cases

Now that we've seen a sample PRD. We are ready to dive deeper into use cases. While engineers will not be writing any use cases from a customer perspective, we will have to understand them because our solution must satisfy the use cases. In fact, while we might not be writing use cases from *end customer perspective*, actually, we will be writing some use cases from a *system* perspective and this is after we've understood the actual customer use cases and requirements. Here's a diagram to depict what you may end up doing.

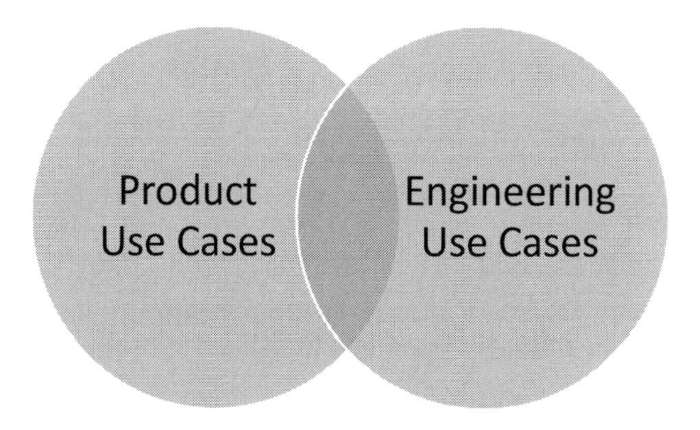

As you can see, product use cases are pretty isolated from engineering use cases because they are on different levels. Product requirements tell WHAT needs to be built, while the engineering requirements tell HOW it needs to be built. The (minimal) area that overlap is where some of the technical details between what a product manager comes up with may be the same as the ones that an engineer would come up with; this is a grey area of specifying use cases and requirements. We don't talk about this grey area much in this book, but you should know that sometimes highly technical product managers may venture deeper than engineers desire or it could be part of the culture of the product team to be highly technical and to be very specific – down to the little detail – about potentially what and how things should work.

In summary, Product Managers author the customer use cases and engineers author the system use cases. By system use cases, we mean the use cases that show how one part of the system that we are building interacts with another part of the system. After all, some Product Manager treats this system as a "black box" and are only concerned about the inputs and outputs. But the engineers are the ones who are building this black box and will need to know how to create this "black box".

Regardless of which use cases exist (end customer or system), there are only three types of use cases that we will be concerned with:

1. Brief
2. Casual
3. Fully Dressed

The table below summarizes the three types. You've seen brief use cases before if you've read UC-001 and UC-002 above with the ice cream machine. Those are brief use cases because they are a few sentences long to a single paragraph in length. The paragraph explains the success scenario (although there are some brief use cases that will explain error scenarios as well). The next type of use case is the casual use case. This casual type is about double to triple the length of a brief use case. They are for use cases that are lengthy or have more detail but without going into every single error or success scenario. Casual use cases usually explain success scenarios as well. Finally, we have the fully dressed use cases. These multi-page use case are complete in each and every way, meaning that it will explain every single success and error scenario in detail. For example, if a user presses the "Order" button, but the ice cream scoop doesn't come out, what should the system do? Imagine all the scenarios that could go wrong, and you have the fully dressed use case.

In all types of use cases, it is imperative to be explicit about who is acting on what. Use cases are all written in words and not diagrammed, so each sentence or phrase in the use case must have a noun and a verb. The noun is usually the person acting on something or could even be the something being acted on. We call this noun the "actor".

All use cases have the following same characteristics:

Brief	Casual	Fully Dressed
• One paragraph long • Usually explains success scenario	• Several Paragraphs long • Usually explains the success scenario	• Many pages long • Contains both success and error scenarios

Actors:

- These are the people, items, or objects that are either acting on something or being acted upon.
- The Primary Actor is the actor who is acting on something. The Primary Actor is like the "leading actor" in a movie, where the movie is about the lead actor.
- The Secondary Actor(s) are the actors who is acted upon by the primary actor or by other secondary actors. The secondary actor is like the "supporting actor" in a movie, where the movie is not really about him/her, but aids in helping the primary actor reach success.

Scenario:

- A use case, regardless of the type, explains one main scenario. A main scenario can have a positive and negative outcomes. A positive outcome is a success scenario. A negative outcome is an error scenario. Therefore, a use case have both success and error scenarios. As we will explain, due the limitations in space and readability (not by readers of this book, but by the readers of the use case), brief and casual type use cases only explain the success scenarios, whereas fully-dressed use cases go into the various corner cases.

2.3.1 Brief Use Cases

Brief use cases are one paragraph long, usually a few sentences of a positive user case scenario. A brief use case is limited by its length. It should clearly identify who the user is, what the user wants to accomplish, and the result of the user's action. It almost always explains a success scenario, except in cases where the brief use case is about an error scenario. UC-001 and UC-002 above are perfect examples of brief use cases.
Brief use cases are used to get an idea across quickly. It can be communicated via speech because of its short form as it's only a few sentences long. Brief use cases are what most project designs start out with, before they are analyzed, prioritized, and fleshed out to become either casual use cases or fully-dressed use cases.
Here's an example of a brief use case involving a mobile phone:

> *User takes her mobile phone out of her pocket and presses the "Ice Cream" app button on her phone. The "Ice Cream" app loads; while loading it presents a loading screen telling her to wait. After loading, the main page of the "Ice Cream" app loads and presents her several options to order ice cream.*

2.3.2 Casual Use Cases

Whereas a brief use case is about a paragraph long. A casual use case is usually more than one to at most three paragraphs long. Usually, they are about two paragraphs. Casual use cases have the same goals as the brief use cases; the only difference is the length. A casual use case is usually a slightly more fleshed out version of the brief use case, meaning that it contains more detail. The detail goes deeper into the user actions as you can see in the example provided below.
Here's an example of a casual use case from the brief use case in the previous section:

We use brief use cases in conversations, casual use cases in lengthier conversations or written documentation, and we use fully-dressed use cases in written documentation.

> *User takes her mobile phone out of her pocket. User unlocks the phone. User finds the "Ice Cream" app button on her phone and presses the icon. The "Ice Cream" app immediately loads.*
> *While loading it presents a loading screen for the duration of the waiting period. The loading screen displays information about the length of time the app will take to load and also some images that showcase the app. The length of time will be depicted by a countdown timer. The images shown will show what users can do with the app and will be displayed for several seconds at a time.*
> *After loading, the main page of the "Ice Cream" app loads. The main page shows the title of the app and several buttons to order ice cream. The buttons are "Order for pickup" and "Order for delivery".*

2.3.3 Fully Dressed Use Cases

When the team decides that a use case is "worthy" for the "fully-dressed" treatment then a lot more energy, effort, and analysis is put into writing a fully-dressed use case. The main differences between a fully-dressed use case and the others we've seen are

(1) the length,
(2) the goals, and
(3) the format.

A fully-dressed use case can be pages long. It can be pages long because it goes into each case in excruciating detail so that there is no room for misinterpretation. The other reason why it can be long are the goals. The goals of the fully dressed use case are to explain both the success and error scenarios. This means that the use case will look like a bulleted list of ifs and what's. Finally, the format is different. No longer is it in paragraph narrative form; it will be a table, with the following several components and template.

Name	Give a descriptive and complete name of the use case. Ex: "UC-1000 Renewing a Library Book using a Mobile App"
Scope	Is this a engineering system level use case or a business use case? Ex: "System Use Case"
Level	Is this a user goal, a sub-function goal, or system goal? "Ex: "System Goal Level"
Primary Actor	Who is the main actor doing the actions? Ex: "Tom, the user of the mobile app"
Stakeholder(s)	Who has influence over the final decisions of the use case? Ex: "Silicon Valley Public Library"
Preconditions	What must occur before the first step of the use case begins? Ex: "The user must have installed the app on his mobile phone"
Postconditions	What must occur after the final success step of the use case? Ex: "The system is updated to reflect the new due date of the book."
Main Success Scenario	What are all the steps from beginning to end that the user does? Ex: See next page.

Extensions	What are all the things that can go wrong with each of the steps in the Main Success Scenario? Ex: See next page.

Here's an example of a "Main Success Scenario". Each step is a single action showing what a user does or what the user experiences.

1. User loads the "Library" app button on her phone and presses the icon.
2. The "Library" app immediately loads.
3. While loading it presents a loading screen for the duration of the waiting period.
4. A dashboard is displayed that shows what users can do with the app: Check Out, Renew Books, Search for Books.
5. User selects Renew Books and is brought to the renew books list screen.
6. User sees a list of books that he has checked out and the associated due dates of each book.
7. User selects the book he wants to renew and the book's title becomes highlighted.
8. User then selects "Renew" button to renew the books.
9. User sees a "Success! Book has been renewed dialog" and clicks Ok.
10. User then sees the updated renew date in the renew books list screen.

Here's an example of an "Extension". This one is when the app crashes at Step #3 above.

3a1. The app crashes while loading.
3a2. The user is asked whether to send a diagnostic report back to our servers so we can diagnose the issue.
3a3. User clicks "Yes" and the diagnostic report is sent back.
3a3a1. User clicks "No" and is brought back to the phone's screen.

Here's another example of an "Extension". This one is when the app is not able to renew the book at Step #9 above.

9a1. User sees "Sorry! The book you selected has been renewed too many times!" and clicks OK.
9a2. The user is brought back to the renew books lists screen to select another book to renew.

We've only shown 2 extensions, but you can imagine an error scenario or even an alternate flow for each of the main success scenario steps. Therefore, the extensions section could be a long section!

2.4 Requirements

Requirements are not use cases. Use cases are not requirements. As we've seen in the previous section on use cases, use cases tell a story about a user and how s/he interacts with the system we wish to build. We've seen many different types of use cases because we use use cases as a medium to communicate our ideas. We use brief use cases in conversations, casual use cases in lengthier conversations or written documentation, and we use fully-dressed use cases in written documentation.

Requirements are atomic facts about what the system should do.

Requirements, on the other hand, are at a lower level than use cases. Requirements are atomic facts about what the system should do. Here are some examples:

a) The user interface must have two buttons.

b) One button must say "Save", and when clicked on, must save the current state of the order.

c) The system must accept a CSV (Comma Separated Values) file as input.

d) The system should never need any batteries or any external power generation as it will self-propel itself.

As an engineer, you won't need to write any requirements, but you should understand it. And if you don't understand it, make sure to clarify with the author of the PRD. **Because it is you, as an engineer, who would need to translate the use cases and its corresponding requirements to the system that you are designing**.

There are 3 things you need to know and get clarity on about requirements:

1) What "must" or "should" be done?

In the examples above, all four requirements either use "must" or "should". Those are some of the most popular keywords to look for as they are keywords that require the system to behave a certain way. If loose words such as "may be" or "may" are used, this is a red flag and clarity should be sought with the author of the PRD. (For more information about the terminology used to specify requirements, see RFC2119).

2) What priority is the requirement?

   Although none of the requirements in the four examples list any priorities, every single requirement should have a priority status. Priority terminology ranges from "High", "Medium", "Low" to other terminology such as "Must have", "Best Effort", or some other demarcations. Regardless of the various terminologies, the intentions are the same. Some requirements "must" be done before the others as they are more important. Some requirements are just there as "wish list" items, which means they don't necessarily have to be done or if time allows, "please get it done".

3) Can it be satisfied? Can I or someone technical design a system that satisfies the requirement?

   This is the trickiest. When you are reading the use cases and requirements, you'll need to read attentively and to a certain degree with some imagination. Let's take a look at the requirement (d) above. Do you think that's possible to implement? Why or why not? (Answer in the footnote[5] below).

2.5 The Design Specification (Intro)

Requirements, just like use cases, fit in our Venn diagram model. The PRD specifies the product requirements but does not specify any engineering requirements. This means that the diagram below, there should be no requirements that are the same between product and engineering requirements[6]. So, given what we've learned so far, we know where the products requirements are located (PRD), but where do the engineering requirements

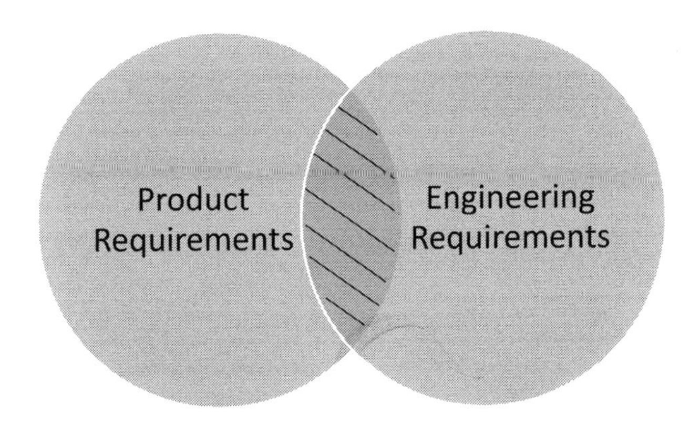

[5] No, the requirement specifies a perpetual motion machine, which according to the law of physics is not possible!

[6] This is partially true. More technical products may have more technical product requirements.

go? We need a place to put our engineering requirements! We can't just take the PRD and starting writing code right?

We call this document:

The **Design Specification**. Technically, yes, you can start writing code whenever you want, but most company process dictates that you document your design so that it becomes maintainable long after you or anyone else has moved on to something else.

We devote an entire chapter to writing a Design Specification in the following chapters.

2.6 Exercises

1. What is a use case?

2. What are the top 3 differences between the 3 types of use cases?

3. Imagine that you would like to introduce an awesome use case to a colleague, should you
    a. Write a fully dressed use case and send it to him over email?
    b. Just tell him the brief use case verbally? or
    c. Send him the PRD.

4. How are product and engineering use cases different?

5. What is a product requirement?

6. What are some questions you should ask yourself when reading a product requirement?

7. As an engineer, what should you do when you review a PRD?

8. How are product and engineering requirements different?

[This page left intentionally blank]

3 DESIGN WITH UML

In this chapter, we will take what we have learned in the previous chapters and start learning and applying UML. The last chapters have given us a better understanding of where things come from and our grounding in software development processes are now much firmer. In this chapter, we will introduce:

> **UML as a way to represent our code from the use cases and requirements before any code gets written.**

3.1 What we know so far

By now, you should be pretty confident in understanding requirements and use cases. We now know what is a problem and what problem we are trying to solve. Because when someone gives us engineers and tells us to "implement that", our response should be, "Ok, let's understand the problem together so I can arrive at a solution that will satisfy what the customer needs". We as engineers should know why what we are doing and for whom. We don't live in the dark because the same information in the PRD which may be corrected and modified by the engineering team to agree on what needs to be built is available to everyone on the team.

Now, it is our job to come up with a design – to create great software – that solves the defined problem and does it as best and as efficiently as possible. It's what we get paid big bucks to do. (As of this writing the average software engineering salary in 2018 with a 4-year undergraduate degree is nearly $100,000 USD compared to an average of $55,000 back in 2000. Salaries for most other types of non-engineering roles have remained relatively the same over the past 20 years.).

This chapter is divided into the following subsections. As always, it's best to go in order.

1. Recap of the two main uses of the ice cream machine that we are building.
2. Translating from use cases and requirements to UML
    a. Introduction to UML
    b. Identifying actors, act-ees, and actions
    c. UML Diagram of our ice cream machine

3.1.1 Use Cases Recap – Analyzing the Use Cases

On the next page is a replica of the use cases and requirements that we reviewed in the previous chapter. We will be using the same two use cases to help us determine how to translate them to UML. We ignore translating use cases to requirements because we assume they are given to us by the Product Manager.

The two use cases are as follows:

UC001 - Setup: The buyer of this ice cream machine would like to be able to set the machine on the table, plug it into a 120-volt outlet, turn it on with a flip of a switch that is easy to reach, and have the ice cream machine ready to use in 15 minutes so that he can start dispensing ice cream to his customers.	UC002 - User order: At the request of the customer who wants strawberry ice cream, the ice cream machine operator presses the strawberry ice cream button first then presses "Order" button. The operator then puts a sugar cone underneath where the scoop of ice cream will come out in 1 minute. A few moments later, the scoop of strawberry ice cream falls onto the cone. The operator takes the cone out and presents it to the customer.

Let's tackle UC001 first. UC001 explains the steps necessary for a user to start using the machine. Who's the user defined in UC001? Is the customer or someone else? UC001 is explained from the perspective of the person setting up the machine. This could be potentially be one of the following users: buyer, customer (buying the ice cream), or a store owner. UC001 specifically states in the first few words that it is the "buyer" so let's assume that this buyer is not the same as the customer. What does the user (buyer) do? He goes through a series of steps, interacting with the machine to get it set up. Specifically, he places the machine on the table, plugs it in, and turns on a switch. That's all he does. How do we translate this into a UML diagram?

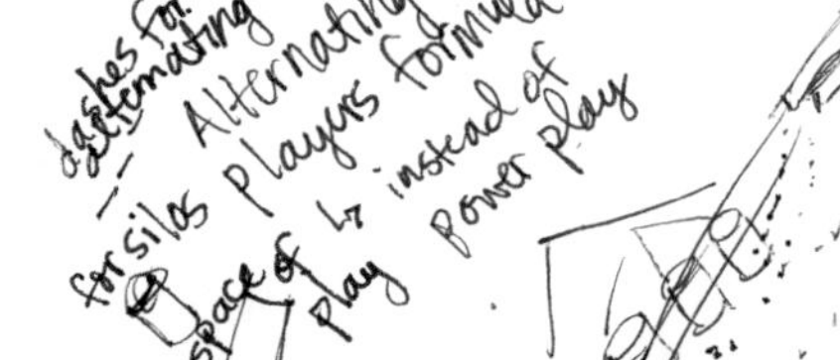

UC001 **cannot** be translated into a *software* UML diagram. UC001 only deals with the hardware aspects of the machine and does not explain what the software does (other than turning on after a flip of the switch). We are missing information about what the software does and because it's missing, we cannot make assumptions as engineers about how it will work. The best thing to do at this point is to continue to read through the PRD to find a use case that addresses what the software will do when it boots up and if we can't find it, ask the Product Manager to clarify.

Since UC001 wasn't very fruitful, we should move on to UC002. Hopefully there is something there for us to do!

What is the difference between UC001 and UC002?

UC002 focuses on the user of the machine, most likely an employee of the ice cream shop who is taking the customer's orders and dispensing the ice cream. There is some information about how the system (or software) works. A button (designated "strawberry") gets pressed, an external action happens where the user puts an ice cream cone into a specific spot in the machine, and then ice cream (strawberry) is dispensed into the cone. That is all we know from the use case. Although we can make some assumptions about the system to be built, we instead should write down a list of questions that we have – questions that help us engineers clarify the use case. Here are some questions that are top of mind (and by no means complete):

- Is there only one button? And that button is for strawberry?
- Are there other flavors? If so, does that mean that will be multiple buttons?
- What if the cone is not there? Would ice cream still come out?
- How long will it take for the ice cream to come out once the button is pressed?
- How long will it take for the ice cream to come out once the cone is inserted into the machine?
- What if there's an error?
    - What if the button fails to respond?
    - What if no ice cream comes out?
    - What if there is no more ice cream left in the machine?

Don't take use cases at face value. There is almost always more to it.

Those are some of the many questions that an engineer might have. UC002 is a use case that is written so high level that we just can't take it face value and design something from it; so, as part of "Analysis" we need to analyze what we as engineers are given so that we can come up with a design that satisfies the requirements.

As part of "Analysis", here's what we do:

- Read and understand the use cases and requirements in the PRD
- When reading the PRD, think and envision what and how you would build the system
- Raise and clarify any questions
- Ask yourself, do all the user steps and processes laid out in the PRD make sense?
- If the answers don't fit what you had originally envisioned, why or why not?

Once you have answered or have answers to the above questions, you will need to ask deeper questions, some of which we will cover in the "Design" phase:

- Does the system even make sense building?
- Does the system described in the PRD already exist in one form or another?
- What subsystems would this system have?

Copy of the Ice Cream Machine PRD Sample

Use Case ID/ Requirement ID	Description	Priority
UC-001	*Setup: The buyer of this ice cream machine would like to be able to set the machine on the table, plug it into a 120-volt outlet, turn it on with a flip of a switch that is easy to reach, and have the ice cream machine ready to use in 15 minutes so that he can start dispensing ice cream to his customers.*	High
REQ-001	The shape of the system must allow it to be placed on a flat table without tipping over.	High
REQ-002	The system must support a 120-volt power plug.	High
REQ-003	The on/off switch should be located in the front of the machine.	High
REQ-004	After the on switch is flipped, the machine must turn on.	High
REQ-005	The machine must be preloaded with ice cream making materials.	High
REQ-006	The machine must be ready to dispense ice cream in 15 minutes.	High
UC-002	*User order: At the request of the customer who wants strawberry ice cream, the ice cream machine operator presses the strawberry ice cream button first then presses "Order" button.. The operator then puts a sugar cone underneath where the scoop of ice cream will come out in 1 minute. A few moments later, the scoop of strawberry ice cream falls onto the cone. The operator takes the cone out and presents it to the customer.*	High
REQ-010	The system must have buttons for each flavor that is offered.	High
REQ-011	The system must have a "Strawberry" flavor button.	High
REQ-012	The system must have an "Order" button, which when pressed, orders the flavor that was most previously pressed.	High
REQ-013	The system must have space to place and hold the ice cream cone.	High
REQ-014	After the order button is pressed, the ice cream scoop must come out within a minute.	High
REQ-015	The scoop must fall onto the ice cream cone. The system must detect that there is an ice cream cone before dispensing the scoop of ice cream.	High
REQ-016	The order button must be painted red color.	Low

3.1.2 Analyzing the Requirements

In 3.1.1, we analyzed the use case. We looked at UC001 and UC002. UC001 was out because it dealt with hardware requirements. UC002 was a very high-level use case and we had a list of questions that we wanted to get clarification on. One thing we didn't do in the previous section is to look at the requirements for UC002 – perhaps it may answer some of our questions!

> REQ-010 states that there are buttons for each flavor! That implies that there are going to be one or more flavors, but it stops short of stating what those flavors are. Let's see if the other requirements answer that question.
>
> REQ-011 states that the "Strawberry" flavor button exists. We knew that from the UC002 so that's not any new additional info.
>
> REQ-012 states that there is a second button "Order" that when you first press the flavor button, you'd have to press the "Order" button in order to execute the order. We also knew that from the UC002 so that's not any new additional info.
>
> REQ-013 jumps[7] to the ice cream cone location and states that there should be space for it. As software engineers, we'll leave this requirement for the hardware people. Let's move on.
>
> REQ-014 states the time (one minute) the ice cream must come out after the order button is pressed. This requirement defines a time element (and a non-functional requirement) to our system meaning that the system we design can't take too long to drop that scoop of ice cream onto the cone. But REQ-014 leaves a question open, what if the user doesn't put a cone? Will the ice cream still have to come out? I assume not.
>
> REQ-015 clarifies our earlier question. The scoop will have to stay ready to be dispensed until it detects a cone. This means that our system must have some sort of mechanism to detect the cone and once detected must perform the action.
>
> REQ-016 jumps back to the buttons, specifically, the order button and states that it has be a particular color (red). We leave this requirement for the hardware engineers.

So, the requirements answered a lot of our questions because that is what it was designed to do! But there are still some questions that are unanswered. You as the engineer will need to get clarity!

Because there is no Product Manager for you to ask, here are the unanswered questions from our list and the answers to those questions:

---

[7] Usually, the requirements are grouped together by parts of what the system does. So, all the requirements for the buttons should be grouped together.

- Is there only one button? And that button is for strawberry?

  ANSWER: REQ-010, REQ-011, and REQ-012 partially answer the question. Unfortunately, there is still lots of data missing. Let me provide you more details:

  There are 3 flavors: Mango, Strawberry, and Chocolate. There will need to be buttons for each of those flavors. There is an ORDER button that only works once a flavor has been selected. If no flavor is selected, then the flavor buttons will flash until one of the flavor buttons are pressed. The flashing tells the user that a flavor must be pressed. Once a flavor button is pressed, the ORDER button flashes to tell the user to press ORDER to finalize the order.

- Are there other flavors? If so, does that mean that will be multiple buttons?

  ANSWER: See response above.

- What if the cone is not there? Would ice cream still come out?

  ANSWER: REQ-015 answers this question.

- How long will it take for the ice cream to come out once the button is pressed?

  ANSWER: REQ-014 partially answers this question. It says about a minute from once the Order button is pressed. But what if it's waiting for the cone to be where it's supposed to be? How long would it take for the ice cream scoop to come out once it detected a cone? Let's assume that once it detected the cone, the scoop will drop onto the cone in 10 seconds.

- How long will it take for the ice cream to come out once the cone is inserted into the machine?

  ANSWER: See answer above.

- What if there's an error?

  - What if the button fails to respond?
  - What if no ice cream comes out?
  - What if there is no more ice cream left in the machine?

  ANSWER: We discussed some scenarios where the buttons would flash in order to alert the user, but we haven't finalized what happens when things go wrong. The error scenarios are not important for our initial UML diagram, so let's ignore for now and let this be an exercise that you can complete at the end of the chapter.

3.2 UML

Before we can proceed to coming up with a design laid out in section 3.1, we are going to learn UML.

UML is a common language used throughout the computer industry (and other industries) to convey and communicate software design. UML stands for Unified Modeling Language. You can use UML to do almost any kind of design/modeling – even including relational database entity relationship diagram. However, our focus is on the software system design so we will only be limiting our scope to the syntax and ideals that compose our diagrams.

3.2.1 UML History

For as long as software or code was invented, there came a need to document how that code works for posterity and/or for whoever assumes ownership of the code in the future. To address this, engineers wrote documentation (usually in text) and diagrams (boxes and pointers) about how the software worked. There wasn't really a "standard" process until software programs became more and more complex and that complexity begat the need to translate what, why, and how things were done for a variety of reasons including but not limited to for compliance, legal, and training.

In approximately year 1996, three engineers from Rational Software (subsequently acquired by IBM) came up with UML to standardize on all the software notations that existed into something called UML that allowed for a single standard way to visualize software.[8] You can probably imagine what software visualization techniques were like pre-1996 where there existed many ways to communicate a design and tireless effort to understand the syntax and notations of all the various methodologies! Although released in 1996, UML (version 2.0) wasn't ratified into ISO (or the International Organization for Standards) until 2005, almost a decade later.

UML has its roots in Object Oriented Programming, which started back in the 1980s. Over the next several decades, UML integrated (and incorporated) many methodologies so that there would be a standard way to diagram and model software visually. UML 2.0 came out in 2008 and serves as the basis of the UML we learn in this textbook.

3.2.2 UML Modern Use Today

Unfortunately, although UML is "popular" there are still some pockets where UML is not heavily adopted. There are two main factors that affect the adoption and learnings of UML: education and company culture.

Most college degree programs in computer science or software engineering include a course on Object Oriented Analysis and Design or Software Engineering. These classes are not always mandatory and unfortunately, some graduates graduate from four-year degree programs and enter the workforce without learning any UML at all. So, there is a subset of students, who are great students, but enter the workforce without knowing UML.

[8] Source: Wikipedia, https://en.m.wikipedia.org/wiki/Unified_Modeling_Language

The second hindrance to the adoption of UML is company culture. For larger companies that emphasize documentation of code for compliance or legal use, UML is usually the language chosen. But this is not always the case as there is no "UML police" to verify whether the diagrams adhere to UML 2.0 standard or not or using some other methodology (such as box and pointer diagrams) to illustrate the design. For smaller companies, who must thrive on moving fast and shipping products and services and may not have documentation as a high priority, they many not adopt UML as readily.

Regardless of the various subsets of people and companies that don't know or don't use UML, most companies utilize UML to various degrees. **So, it is important that YOU know UML because when the chance comes for you to show your skills as a software engineer or architect, you will have it at your disposal.**

3.2.3 UML Syntax

UML diagrams consists of boxes, called classes, and lines connecting them, called associations. In this section, you will learn the main syntax of UML and by the end of this chapter, you should be able to diagram simple UML diagrams.

3.2.3.1 UML Classes

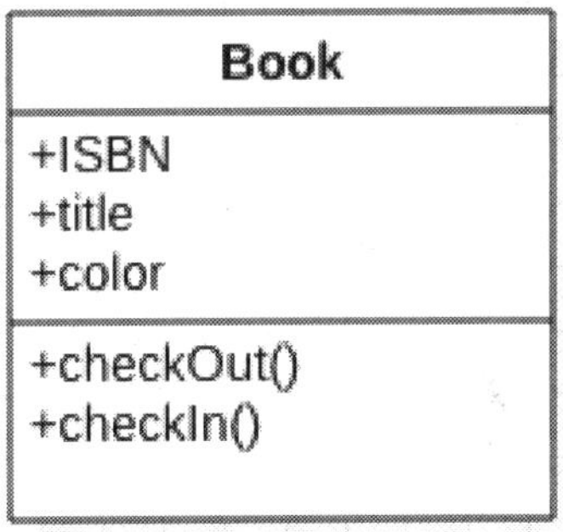

On the right is a diagram of a "Book" class. A class is an entity or a concept. It is a noun. In UML, a class is represented by a box. Inside the box is the contents of the class.

Book
+ISBN +title +color
+checkOut() +checkIn()

A class has three components that are separated by lines within the class diagram box:

- title of the class,
- attributes, and
- methods (also called operations).

In "Book", we see that the title of the class is "Book". There are three attributes: ISBN, title, and color. There are two methods: checkOut() and checkIn(). These attributes and methods fully describe the Book class. You can take the diagram and convert it directly into object-oriented code, which we will do in the next section.

Attributes are properties of the class. They are "state" that describes the class. The official format is the following:

```
VISIBILITY NAME: TYPE [MULTIPLICITY] = DEFAULTVALUE
{ PROPERTY-STRING}
```

VISIBILITY means whether the attribute is “public” or “private”, denoted by “+” or “-“ respectively.
NAME is the attribute name, which is an array of characters.
TYPE is the system type of the variable. This could be a primitive or another class.
MULTIPLICITY is the number of times or range of numbers that this particular class’s attribute can occur.
DEFAULTVALUE is the assigned default value when the attribute is created.
PROPERTY-STRING defines whether the properties of this attribute, where the values can be user defined.

Let's look at a real example to put this all into context.

+ foo: String [1] = "bar" {readOnly}

The first character of the example is the "+" symbol. It stands for "public", meaning that this attribute can be seen directly by other classes without calling getter and setter methods. The next set of characters is the name of the attribute, which is "foo". Foo is a type String. Foo can only exist once. Foo's default value is the string "bar". Foo cannot be modified because it's read only.

The methods, just like the attributes, are represented similarly. Here's the formal UML format:

VISIBILITY NAME (parameter-list) : return-type {property-

VISIBILITY, NAME, and PROPERTY STRING have the same definition as attribute format. The Parameter-List is the list of parameters that the method accepts. The Return-Type is the type of output.

Let's look at another real example to put this all into context.

+ changeName(in x:String, in y:int, out z:char) : null

The method's name is changeName. It's a public method, meaning that this method can be called directly by other classes. changeName accepts 3 parameters as input, one of which is an output parameter. Technically, the output of the method is "null", meaning that it doesn't return anything. However, there is a parameter called "z" that does get modified, but not officially the output of the method. Two parameters "x" and "y" are the input parameters. The property-string is left out of the example.

As you can see, there is a "formal" definition and format and there is casual use. This book uses both cases to illustrate points when needed. It will be up to you and your workplace whether you want to follow the formal definition or not, because if it's well understood, then you don't need to document every little detail, as it will complicate the diagram. So, in my example, it is perfectly fine to say "checkIn()" and "checkOut()", without adding the formalities of visibility, return type, and other pieces of information that may pollute the diagram.

3.2.3.2 UML Associations

Associations describe a relationship between two different classes. Why do we want to establish relationships among classes? We want to document how classes are related to each other, if at all. Classes that are related to each other use one another's methods and attributes. It shows a relationship that directly ties the two classes together. Indirect relationships do not have associations.

Three components compose an association.

- Name
- Multiplicity (optional)
- Type

The name of the association is usually a one word or phrase that characterizes the relationship between two classes. Examples are usually verbs such as "Author **writes** Book", where the name of the association would be "write".

The multiplicity tells how many instances of the object can be instantiated. See the box below for an explanation of multiplicity.

There are five (5) different types of associations:

- Dependency
- Directional
- Bidirectional
- Aggregation, and
- Composition.

Each type of association has different characteristics and it's important that you know when to use them. I have ordered the associations above, from Dependency to Composition (top to bottom), to emphasize weakest to strongest types of associations. Dependency is the weakest type of association, while Composition is the strongest. On the next page, we look at each type and analyze why some are weak links and some are stronger.

Multiplicity

As we will see, certain types of Associations may have numbers at each or either end of an association. The numbers specify the multiplicity, meaning how many instances of that object can be instantiated. All multiplicity have a lower and upper bound specified by the "m..n" notation, where m is the lower bound and n is the upper bound. The default is 1.

The "*" notation means many. This notation is the same as "0..*", which means zero or more instances.

The "1..*" notation means at least one instance.

A number such as "5" means only 5 instances.

A set of numbers such as 3, 4, 10 means only
3, 4 or 10 instances.

In the example below, there is an association between Author and Book. Here's how you read it.

- The book has many authors (denoted by the "*" on the right side of the association).
- The Author has written at least one book. (denoted by the 1..* on the left side of the association).

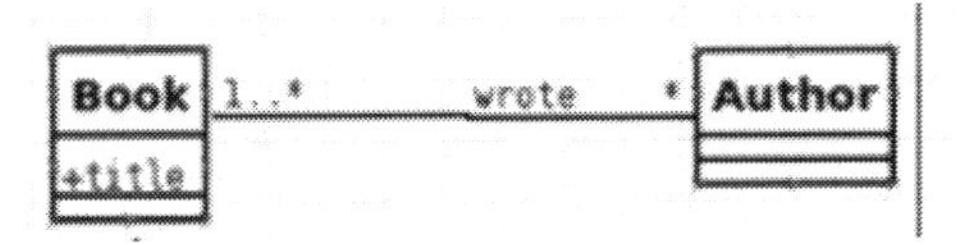

Dependency Association

Dependency association is the weakest type of association because all it shows is that one class "uses" another class. By "use", we mean a simple reference. So, in the example below with classes Book2 and Author2, Book2 is dependent on Author2 because in the method authorExists, it uses the Author2 class. In terms of objects, we say that the Author2 object is used by an object of another class Book2.

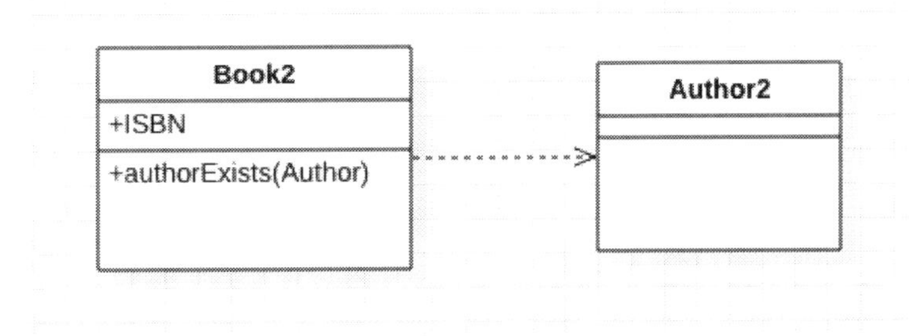

Side Note: We usually don't need to add Dependency associations as it pollutes the diagram especially when there are other types of associations that we want to convey as they are stronger relationships and have side effects.

Directional Association

Directional association is stronger that dependency association. The reason why it's stronger is that the attribute stores state of the referenced class. So, in the example below with classes Book3 and Author3, Book3 is directionally associated to Author3 because in the attribute authors, its type is Author3. In terms of objects, we say that Book3 object stores object(s) of another class Author3.

Notice that we've added multiplicity as well to the association. As an example, we do this to describe that a Book3 object must have at least one or more authors, and that Author3 object can belong to as many Book3 objects.

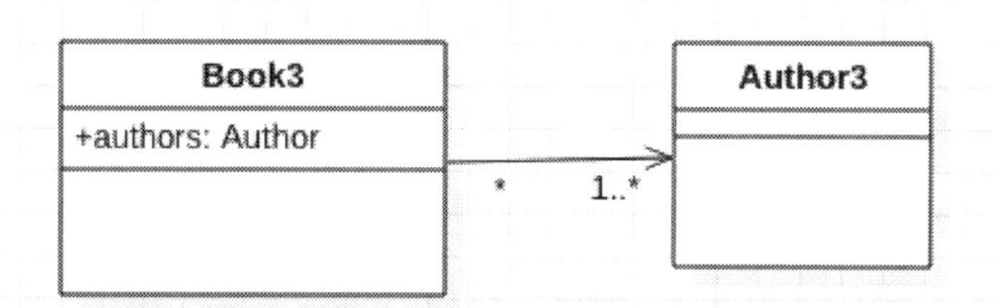

Side Note: Similarly, to Dependency association, we usually don't need to add Directional associations as it pollutes the diagram especially when there are other types of associations that we want to convey as they are stronger relationships and have side effects.

Bidirectional Association

Bidirectional association are the most common type of associations as they are easiest to draw (no arrows) and easiest to start learning UML relationships as it does not impose any referenceable direction. But that is not to say that all your associations should be bidirectional! There are 5 different types of associations for a reason!

Bidirectional means that the "arrows" reference both sides, and because it does, we drop the arrows when drawing the association so it simplifies the diagram. In the example below, the Book class is associated with the Author class using the bidirectional association type. There is a line segment that connects to the two boxes

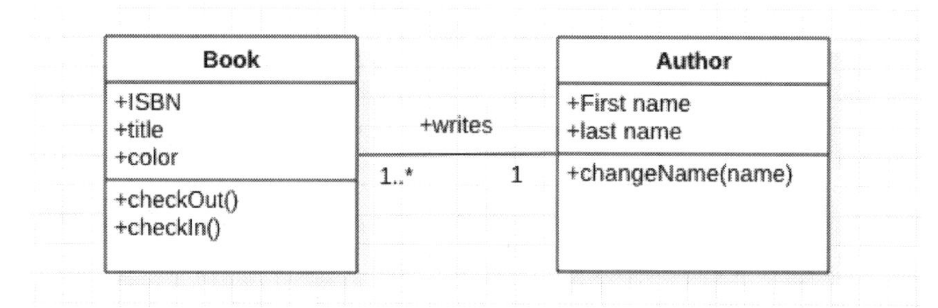

and there is a name of the association called "writes". We say that the Author writes Book. This establishes a relationship and names the relationship (writes).

Side Note: Notice in the example that we've purposefully left out the methods and attributes that reference each other. Although we should technically add them to our diagram, we don't add them if it's well understood because it may pollute the diagram unnecessarily. I think you are starting to get the hint that we only document/diagram things that are super important and we leave minute details that are unnecessary or given out of the diagram for simplicity.

Aggregation Association

Aggregation is a stronger type of bidirectional association. Aggregation association is used when you want to have a child that can exist independently of the parent. If you have Kindergarten class and a Student class where the Student class is a child of the Kindergarten class, when you remove the Kindergarten class, the Student(s) can still exist. Using the Book/Author example, let's extend the diagram by adding a new class called "Shelf". Shelf "aggregates" the books. If Shelf is deleted, the books on the shelf will remain. This is depicted in the diagram below.

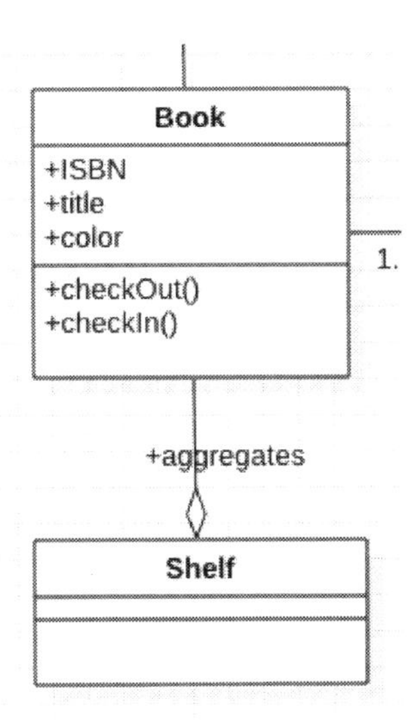

Side Note: Bidirectional, Aggregation, and Composition associations are almost always depicted i.e. you don't want to express an aggregation relationship as a bidirectional relationship, so it's crucial that when you do decide to depict the association, you do so correctly especially with the strong types of associations.

Composition Association

Similarly, Composition is a specific case of association. However, Composition association is used when the child cannot exist independently of the parent. So, if you have a Bathroom class and a Toilet class where the Toilet is the child of the Bathroom class, when you remove the Bathroom, the Toilet(s) will also be removed since toilets cannot exist independent of the Bathroom.

Extending the Book example, let's purposefully add a composition relationship to Book by adding a new class called "Volume". Let's say Volume's job is to compose of all the books because we are saying that a set of books makes a volume. Then, the diagram below depicts the Volume and Book composition relationship. Now, if Volume is deleted, then Books will also be deleted since we are saying that Books cannot exist independent of Volume (in real life, books can exist outside of a volume, but we are using this example for illustrative purposes).

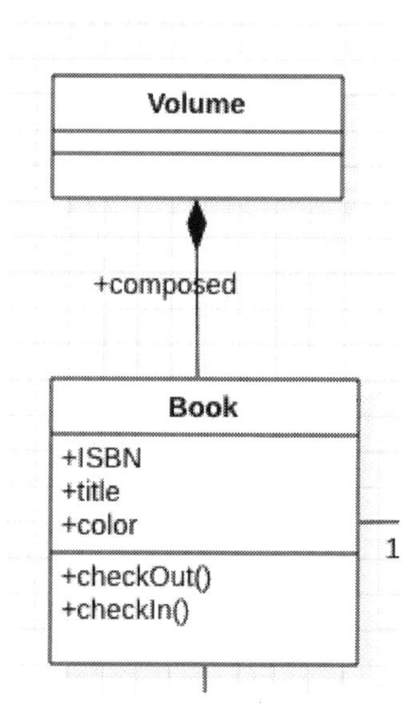

When should you use Aggregation vs Composition?

Are there any hard or fast rules? It depends on what you want to accomplish in your diagram. If you are looking for a "contained in" relationship or when you want the parent to "own" the child, then go with Composition. But if you want the child to be standalone, then you should use the Aggregation association.

Inheritance

One of the key properties of Object-Oriented design is the ability to generalize by inheriting properties from another class. Inheritance is denoted using the association with the empty arrow pointing to the general class. So, in the example to the right, we say that Book inherits from a class called Item.

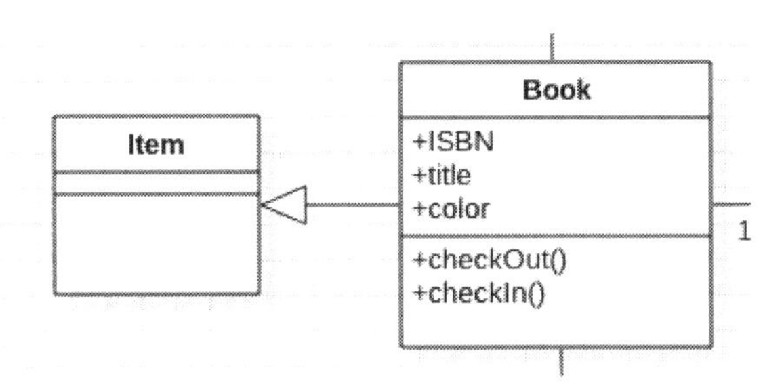

Interface

A class can implement an interface. An interface specifies properties and methods signatures, but they don't have the actual method bodies so the implementing class must provide them. Interfaces are great for contracts between two or more teams working together on different components but the code must "interface" or work with each other via a common face, which is called the interface. As an example, API, or Application Programming Interface, is a terminology to describe a certain type of interface.

In the example below, we have an Interface called "AllItems" that has two methods that would need to be implemented by Book and Magazine, since they both have an interface relationship.

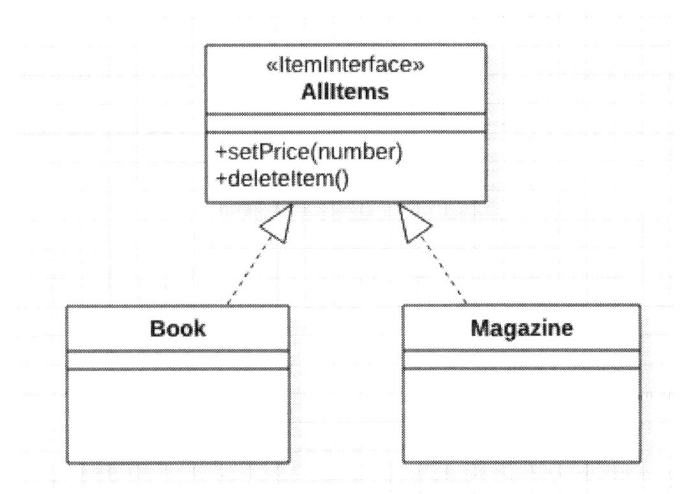

3.2.3.3 UML Summary

Let's review the components of the UML diagram and place them into one diagram as shown below. The diagram below shows 3 different associations (Composition, Bidirectional, and Aggregation) and Generalization (specifically, Inheritance). We have arbitrarily added multiplicity to the Bidirectional association and added some attributes and operations/methods. Now, let's use this diagram and translate this into code in the next section.

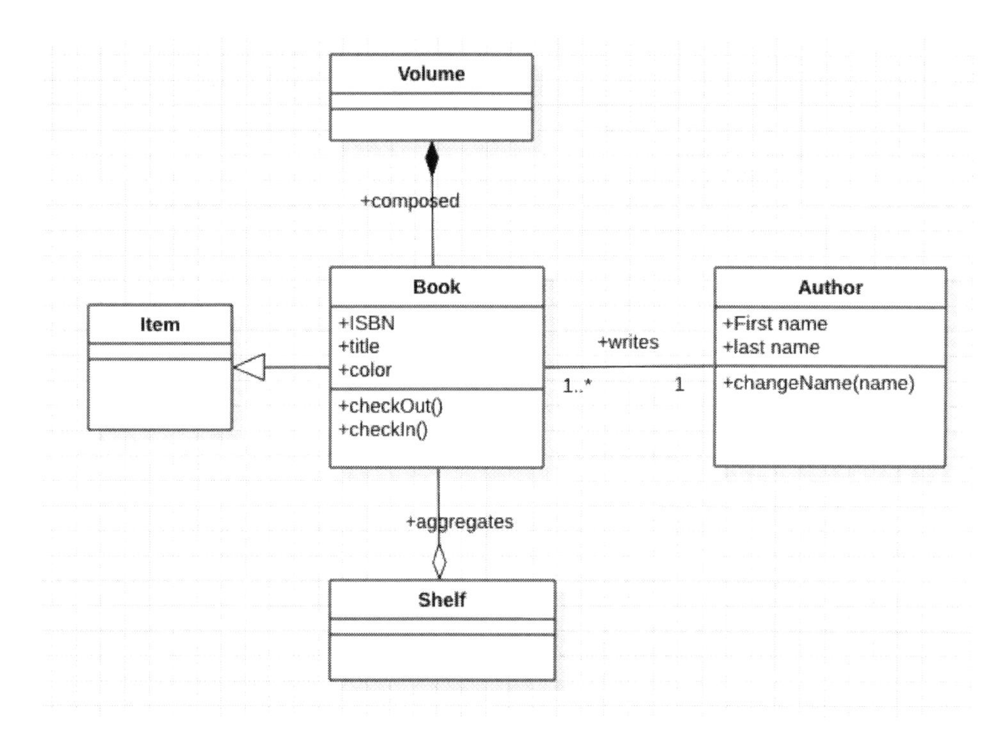

3.3 UML to Code

Using the UML diagram in the previous section, we want to convert it directly to code. UML allows us to do this and it is a pretty straightforward translation.

You can either do this yourself manually or if you used a UML diagram software such as StarUML or Eclipse IDE, you can download plug-ins that allow you to automatically generate code from the UML diagram into any programming language that you choose.

Suppose we want to do this manually. What should be the first steps?

- Translate the classes/interfaces first that have the least associations until all classes in the diagram have been translated. You may also want to start with the classes that have the weakest type of association until you get to the strongest types of association. You will need to make assumptions as you work, keep track of the assumptions, and verify that those assumptions are correct when you are nearing completion.

Why do we want to start translating with the weakest association? We want to start with the "leaf" classes because they have the fewest and weakest type of dependencies. This allows us to focus on the class itself, instead of worrying about how this class relates to another.

In the UML diagram, which one should we start out with? Item superclass looks like a good candidate since it acts a super class of Book. Next, we want to work on Author, then Shelf, then Volume. Last, we want to work on Book. (This is only a recommendation. As you get more experience, you may tackle the problem in any order that you choose).

Now, let's write the Item class code in Java. The UML diagram didn't have any attributes or operators listed, so we leave it empty in the code for illustrative purposes. Starting out with this class was a good decision since the result is so simple:

```
class Item {
      // body of the class goes here
}
```

Below is the Author class code in Java. As you can see, it's a direct translation from the properties and operations into code. You may be wondering how did we know the types of the attributes and methods because the UML diagram didn't say? In this case, since the UML diagram was silent on the types, we had to make the best educated guess. When the code is autogenerated, the program will most likely select "void" as the return type unless you explicitly add a type.

```
class Author {
      String firstName;
      String lastName;

      void changeName(String name) {
      }
}
```

Below is the Shelf class and shows the code for Aggregation between Book and Shelf. For Aggregation, when Shelf is deleted, the books don't die because the Book objects that get added to the list are not created within Shelf, they are created externally. In this example, the Book objects are added via a method called addBooks(Book).

```
class Shelf {
        List books;

        public Shelf () {
                books = new List();
        }

        boolean addBooks(Book b) {
                books.add(b);
        }
}
```

Volume and Book have a composition relationship because the Book objects are created inside the Volume object. In the example below, the Book objects are created right before they are added inside a method called addBooks(bookname). Compare and contrast the Volume and Shelf class - do you see any differences?

```
class Volume {
        List books;

        public Volume () {
                books = new List();
        }

        boolean addBooks(String bookname) {
                Book b = new Book(bookname);
                books.add(b);
        }
}
```

Finally, we have the Book class. Book's super class is Item, so we have to make sure it inherits from the Item class. There are three attributes and two operations. We've added a specific constructor class because we assumed in Volume that Book would take as input a bookname when creating a new instance. The body of the two operations are left blank.

```
class Book extends Item {
      String ISBN;
      String title;
      Color color;

      public Book (String name) {
            this.title = name;
      }

      boolean checkIn() {
      }

      boolean checkIn() {
      }
}
```

However, we made a mistake because we didn't account for the multiplicity between Book and Author. There are two relationships that we want to capture:

1. Book must have one Author.
2. An Author must write one or more Books.

We will need to make changes to both the Book and Author classes.

```
class Book extends Item {
      String ISBN;
      String title;
      Color color;
      Author author;

      // Adding Author as a parameter to the
constructor forces Book to always accept an
Author at creation time.
      public Book (Author a, String name) {
            this.author = a;
            this.title = name;
      }

      boolean checkIn() {
      }

      boolean checkIn() {
      }
}
```

```
class Author {
      String firstName;
      String lastName;
      List books = new List();

      // Forcing Author's constructor to accept Book as a parameter
would create a circular dependency. So instead, we use a setter method.
      public Boolean setBook(Book b) {
            if (b == null) {
                  throw new IllegalArgumentException("Author must have
at least one book!");
            } else {
                  books.add(b);
            }
      }

      void changeName(String name) {
      }
}
```

3.4 UML Class Diagram Limitations

UML class diagrams are great. It's easy to understand visually and it's relatively easy to translate to code. This is why there are programs written to automatically take as input a UML diagram and convert it to code that you can actually use to complete your work. And that's where it ends because there's a lot more code that you have to write.

Let's discuss four main limitations of UML class diagrams.

- Don't tell you how the methods are implemented. Remember, we had to do this ourselves. UML class diagram will give us the interfaces and contracts to use the class such as the exposed methods, but it doesn't contain the body of the methods.
- Only show you high level view of the system. We don't want to document or diagram every single part of our system in UML. We only want to diagram the important parts. Diagraming every single part of the overall system would be overkill. So, UML class diagrams can give us a high-level overview of the system and detailed view of the area(s) of focus.
- Diagraming space is limited. Yes, sometimes we wish that we had infinite amount of paper or whiteboard space. The truth is that space is limited and that limits what we can put in our UML class diagram before it gets too complex and complicated to decipher what is going on. This emphasizes that we only want to diagram what is important.
- It's static, meaning that it only offers a snapshot view. We don't know "how" it works or any sequence of calls. In the next chapter, we will explore other types of UML diagrams that provide us the dynamic view: UML Sequence Diagrams.

3.5 UML Software

There are many different computer software that you can use to draw your UML diagrams. There is no perfect tool to do it. I'm listing a few tools that have gained popularity over the years; by no means am I endorsing any of the software below. Before you venture out and start drawing UML on the computer, my advice is to draw the UML on paper first – get comfortable on paper – and then use the software.

Below is a small list of UML software that I have used and have worked for me. You may find this information useful or you may find other tools that also fit your need. If you do, please feel free to reach out to me so I can update this list.

- StarUML (http://staruml.io)
- Visio (http://microsoft.com)
- Draw.io (http://draw.io)
- Eclipse (http://eclipse.org)
- Dia (https://sourceforge.net/projects/dia-installer/

[This page left intentionally blank]

3.6 Exercises

1. What is UML?

2. Who is UML for?

3. What makes UML so important in the workplace?

4. What are all the types of Associations?

5. What is the difference between the 5 different types of Associations?

6. Draw a UML diagram for a simple table that has a table top and 4 legs.

7. Draw a UML diagram for a simple chair that has a back, seat, and 4 legs.

8. In #6 and #7, combine the diagrams. How can you make your UML diagram more object oriented?

9. Draw a UML diagram for a simple desk that has a desktop, 2 drawers, and 4 legs. How similar is this to your diagrams in #6 and #7.

10. Combine #6, #7, and #9 into one UML diagram and make the UML diagram most object oriented and efficient as possible.

[This page left intentionally blank]

4 Other Types of Artifacts

UML class diagrams are great ways to represent what your system is, but it doesn't provide a complete picture of what's going on in the system. Fortunately, engineers have devised ways to represent where the system fits, what the system does, and how the system does it.

So far, we have used UML to diagram "what the system does", and specifically we used UML Class Diagrams. We used boxes to represent the classes and the lines to represent how the different classes are associated with each other. From the UML class diagram, we were able to figure out what the system does, meaning what the various components and methods that need to be built in order to make it a reality. UML is like a blueprint for building a house. From the UML class diagrams we can translate them into code similar to how we can translate a blueprint of a house to build the house. After all, you can't execute a UML diagram! But you can surely execute code!

But there are many other types of diagrams that we need to learn because having a "static" view of the system is insufficient for us. UML class diagrams provides us only a static view of the system. Architecture diagrams provide us another "static" view of the system, but allows us to see the larger picture and where our system under development fits into the grand scheme of things. Alternatively, we also want to know what the system does over time, which gives us a "dynamic" view of the system. Sequence diagrams provide us that "dynamic" view.

In this chapter, we will dive into two main types of diagrams: **Architecture Layer Diagrams (ALD), Architecture Flow Diagrams (AFD),** and **Sequence Diagrams**. With those four types of diagrams under our belt (UML Class, Architecture Layer and Flow Diagrams, and Sequence Diagrams), we will be able to put together a Software Functional Specification or Design Specification of our system.

4.1 Architecture Layer Diagram

Imagine if we wanted a bigger picture view - a zoomed out view of what we are doing. What if we wanted to take a step back and ask "Where is this house that we are building located?", then the UML class diagram will not be able to answer that question because the UML class diagram only gives us the blueprint of the house, not where the house is located in the neighborhood. Thus, a new type of diagram called the Architecture Layer Diagram (or ALD. We use "layer" to differentiate from an Architecture *Flow* Diagram) was invented to satisfy the problem.

An ALD provides the entire big picture view of the system and its relationship with the operating system and any application(s) that rely on it. So instead of a blueprint, the ALD is basically a map of the neighborhood. You can't build a house with a map of a neighborhood, but you use it to find the house!

ALD are important in that they give the bigger picture view of how your system fits into the overall system. Whatever you design, whether it's an operating system or just a small application or a module that does anything in the system, an ALD provides that high level view.

Realizing that the ALD is important, how do we get started? First, let's go into the principles in drawing an architectural diagram.

How to draw an Architectural Layer Diagram - Principles to Follow

1. Each "module" in the diagram should be a rectangular box.
2. A "module" is a specific part of the system.
3. Where a module is located in the diagram matters.
4. Applications are usually depicted at the top of the diagram as applications as they are considered higher level components.
5. An operating system (OS) is usually depicted as the lowest of the diagram as the operating system sits right above the hardware. Software that sits right above the hardware is considered lowest level components.
6. Between the operating system and the applications are usually the libraries, whether they are system libraries from the operating system, other systems such as middleware or infrastructure, or libraries or other software in general that your system may require.
7. You only want to depict the modules that your system depends on because a system could have over 1000 modules (or some insane amount) and not all of them are going to be relevant to the software you are writing.
8. Libraries are software that other people have already written. You will only depict specific libraries if your system relies on it.
9. Keep the diagram as clean as possible without making it overly complex but also not overly simple.

4.1.2 Ice Cream Machine (ICM) Architecture

Let's go through a real example with the Ice Cream Machine! How would you diagram the architecture layers for the Ice Cream Machine? Take a moment to draw this out and come back to this section in a few minutes.

Here's how you would tackle this problem in a step-by-step way.

A. **Step 1** - Determine the input's and out's of the system.
   This means look at any data or input or output that the system requires or completes. We know the ICM accepts ice cream materials and human input as inputs and the finished ice cream product as output. This is important to know because we want to be sure if there is a human involved so we can draw that human interface as one of the modules and the ice cream materials as one of the other modules. Said in another way, it's important to understand any system as a black box first before diving into the details.

   Input (Material) #1: ICM accepts materials needed to make ice cream.
   Input (User input) #2: ICM accepts human input to take orders.
   Out: (Ice cream) #1: ICM creates the ice cream on a cone.
   Output (Notifications) #2: ICM may decide to notify the user if things go wrong.

B. **Step 2** - Draw a large box that depicts the ICM. This large box is the software that you write. It will sit on top of some operating system and will use libraries. But let's just draw the "blackbox" that we analyzed in Step 1.

C. **Step 3** - Draw where the OS is located. Let's say, as an example, the operating system in Linux. Linux will be the OS of our ICM as it acts as the interface between the code that we write and the hardware required to make the ice cream. Now our diagram has two boxes.

D. **Step 4 -** Draw where the libraries are located, if any. Let's also say we will use the Java JRE (Runtime to execute Java code) library because the code is written in Java. So then, you have a diagram that looks like this. Let's add one more library, and I know this use case we didn't talk about, but let's say we want to allow the machine to take orders over Bluetooth. Let's say someone walks up to the machine, opens up a mobile app, and instead of connecting to the Internet, which could be down, uses the Bluetooth signal of the machine and phone instead to connect. So, we will want to add a Bluetooth library to the diagram*. now our diagram has 4 boxes. We are getting somewhere!

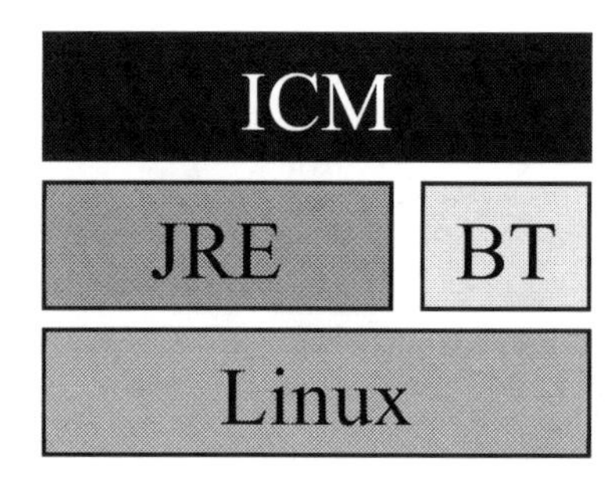

**JRE comes with a Bluetooth library, so if your design uses it directly and not the operating system's version, then technically the [BT] module resides inside the JRE module. So, you can also draw it like this:*

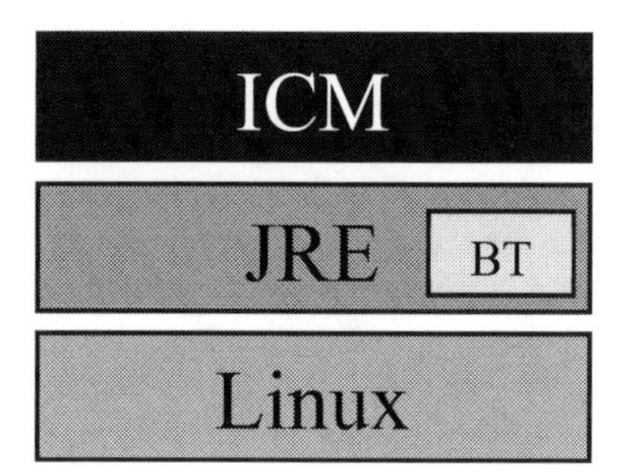

E. **Step 5** - Zoom into Step #2 and break that large box that you drew into smaller modules. Now that we have identified all the peripheral modules that our ICM depends on, let's actually go into the box that we drew in Step #2 and divide the ICM into its parts. These are the modules that have important functions in your system. I have an example architecture layer diagram on the next page. If your diagram does not look like mine, that's ok. The next subsection talks about how to know what module to draw.

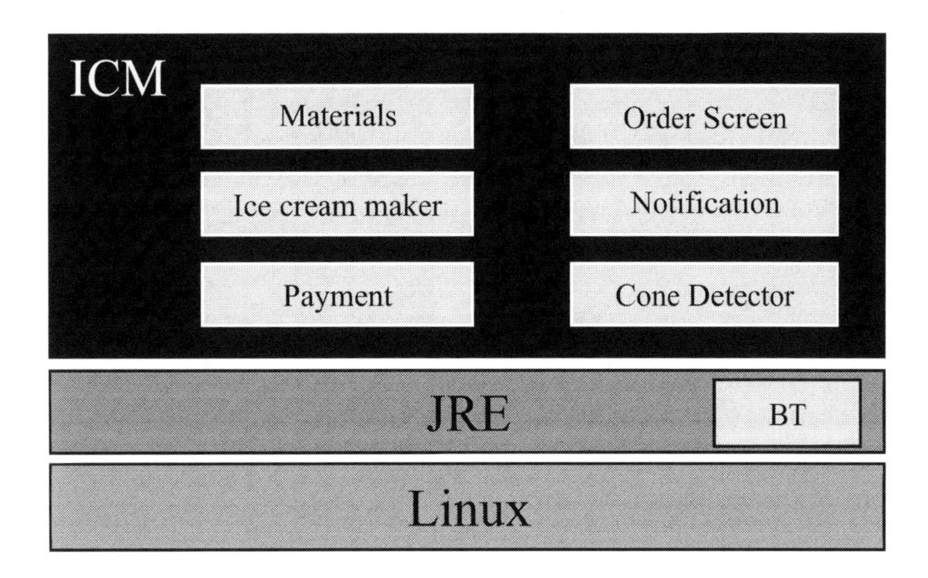

We listed 6 different modules in our system: materials acceptor, order screen, ice cream maker, payment, notification system, and the cone detector. We think those are the most important modules in our system because we need something that accepts the materials, something to accept orders through a screen system, something to accept payment, something to notify the customer if something is wrong or right, something to make the ice cream and something to detect the cone so that the scoop of ice cream scoop can be placed on it. Those look like reasonable modules to me. Let's take this at face value and move on, fully knowing that we may decide to either add or remove modules in the future.

F. **Step 6** - Check your diagram. Finally, we are done! After we check each module, we want to ask ourselves whether we have diagramed the right level of detail. We don't want to diagram single lines of code or APIs. We want to diagram only the modules of the system that do important functions and that we think helps other engineers (or whoever is looking at your architectural diagram) understand your design.

So far so good. Our diagram in Step 5 looks good. However, is there some way that we can reorder the modules in ICM so that there is a more natural ordering? We want modules that interface with the customer closer to the customer (top) and modules that interface with the other external subsystems closer to the bottom. If we can do that, then I think our diagram will look a lot more sensical!

Now look at the new diagram below. What did we do? At first glance, we extended the size of some modules, reordered the ones that look like they are closest to the user, and moved the ones that the user doesn't see further away from the top.

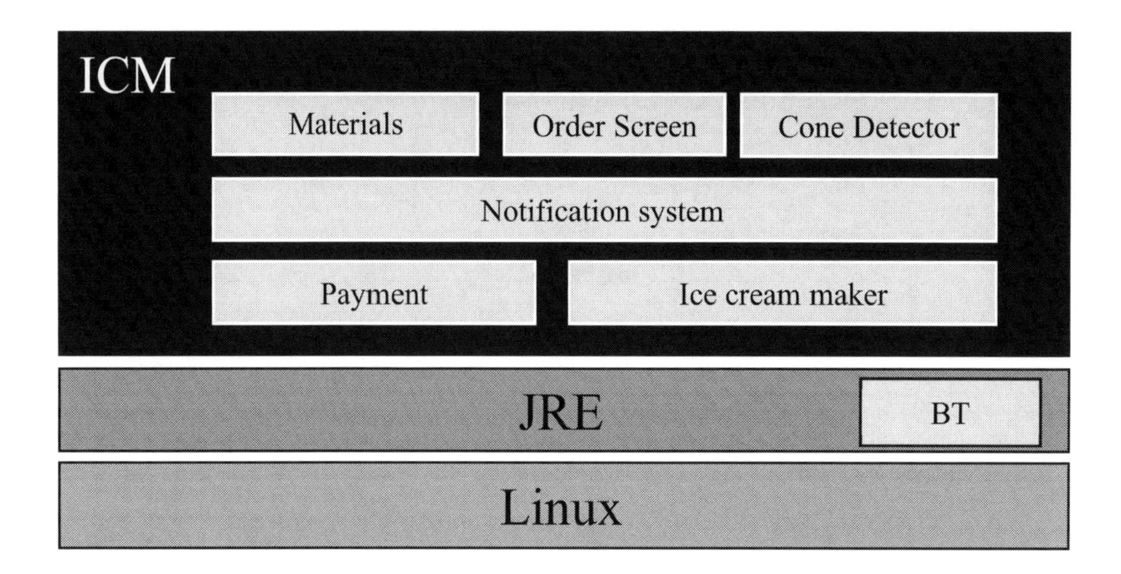

Let's dive deeper. We reordered Materials Acceptor, Order Screen, and Cone Detector to the top because those are modules that we feel interface directly with the user. The employee inputs the materials to make ice cream. The customer uses the order screen to order or get notified. The employee places the cone in the machine and the cone detector detects it. Those three make sense to place at the top inside the ICM box.

We extended Notification System because this is a module that touches almost every single other module. We envision using the notification system as a way to pass messages from one module to another so that if there is something wrong with payment, the notification system acts as a conduit and passes the message to the order screen to alert the user. You can apply this same principle to determine why with the modules materials acceptor and cone detector as an exercise at the end of the book.

Our ALD looks clear and concise. It gives the right amount of detail without being overly complex. It's clear what the main modules in the system are and it's clear what external items that ICM depends on. It also doesn't add extraneous items to the diagram. I think we can call it a day!

4.1.3 Commonly Asked Questions about ALD

How do I know what module to draw in the system?

A module is not necessarily equivalent to a single class. A module may be a collection of classes. A module is a function of the system.

There are many ways to answer this question and ultimately it will depend on who the audience is who will be consuming the diagram. As we said before, we want to draw a box for each module that we find important in the system. Well, what does "important" mean? Does it mean a class in my UML diagram? Important is a very arbitrary term and there is no straight answer. The module could be one class or a collection of classes, it doesn't matter, as long as the module serves a specific important function. What does the module do? Module A processes the user input. Module B converts user input to a set of instructions for the machine. Module C takes the ice cream materials and instructions and measures the right amount of materials to use. Module D takes the calculated materials and creates the ice cream per the set of instructions. Module E presents the completed ice cream so that the user can grab it. Modules A through E would be depicted as different boxes in the diagram.

How do I diagram how modules interact with each other?

ALD don't have arrows. Instead they use the layered approach to diagram interactions. If a module is stacked above another module, then there is an implicit interaction between the two. However, we don't know the direction(s) of the interaction.

How do I show the Internet for cloud-based systems?

Here's one example showing a client and server relationship over the internet. The client is our ICM architecture. The Server is an online payment processor.

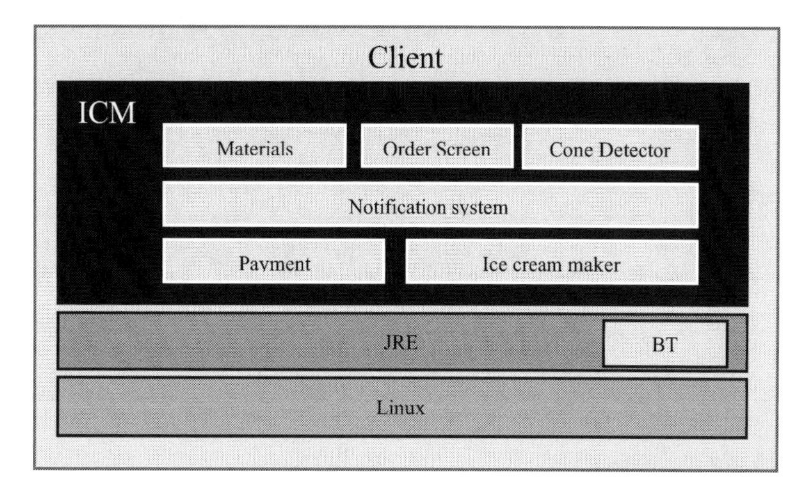

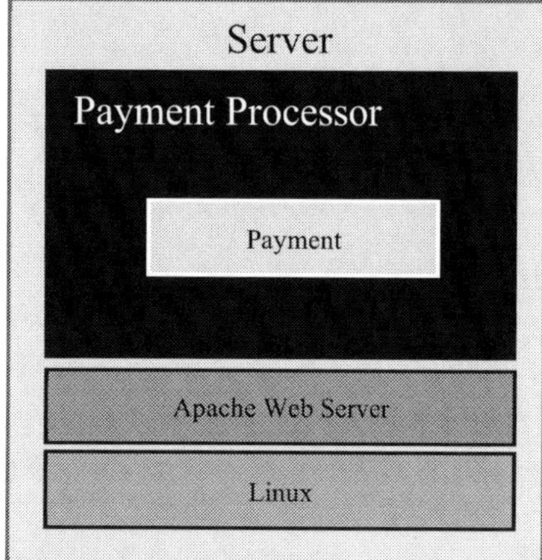

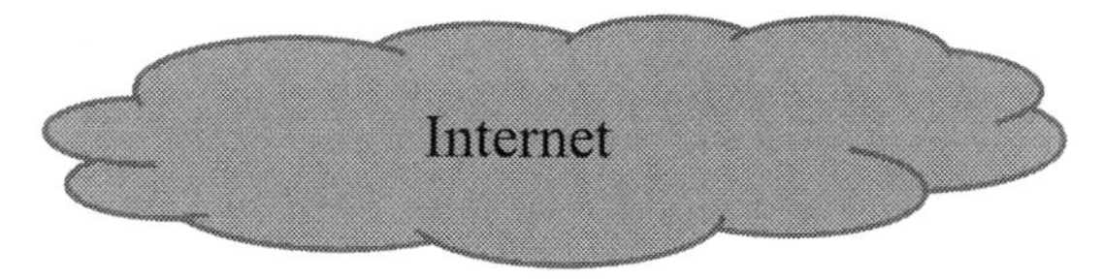

4.2 Architecture Flow Diagram

Slightly different than an Architecture Layer Diagram, where we focused on the individual layers of the system for the entire system, for the AFD (or Architecture Flow Diagram), we focus on just the system under development itself. We will draw the important modules just like we did in when doing ALD, but we will leave out higher level concepts such as the operating system, libraries, etc. The goal of the AFD is to show just the system under development and its various modules interact with each other. You can say that an ALD is a higher-level view than an AFD.

Here are the steps to draw an AFD:

A. Determine who are the users of the system. We call them **actors**.
B. Determine the most important **modules** you want to show. The modules can be borrowed from the ALD diagram. In some cases, it is a straight copy and paste. But in most cases, you may want to go deeper and show databases and networking as examples.
C. Determine how the **actors interact with the modules**.
D. Determine how the **modules interact with each other**.

Let's draw the AFD for the ice cream machine.

First, we have two actors in the system. We have the employee and we have the customer. Employee only interfaces with the system by pouring in the materials. Customer interacts with the machine via the screen, the payment interface, and the slot to put in the cone.

Second, for the modules, we have already done the work as ALD has provided us a good number and relevant modules that we can use. Do we need to add more? Not in this example; we have all our bases covered so far.

Third, we don't exactly know how the actors interact with the modules, but we discussed that when we talked about the actors. We said: *"We have the employee and we have the customer. Employee only interfaces with the system by pouring in the materials. Customer interacts with the machine via the screen, the payment interface, and the slot to put in the cone."* Those two lines tell us that the employee interacts with the Materials Acceptor, perhaps not directly, but the concept is true. This module may be called something else in the future or a fancier name. But for the purposes of this example, let's stick with Materials Acceptor name. Next, the customer interacts with three different modules: the screen, the payment interface, and the slot to put in the cone. Let's draw arrows showing the interactions. We can use single direction or bidirectional arrows to show the direction of interaction.

Fourth, we need to determine how the modules work together. We know that the Notification System serves as the "brain" or message passing interface of our machine, so let's place that in the middle of the diagram. We additionally know there should be arrows going from all the other modules to the Notification System. In most cases, the arrows are bidirectional, such as the case with the Order Screen, Payment, Cone Detector, and Ice cream maker. Order Screen relays the information from the notification system and also adds information from the user input. Similarly, Payment takes in the customer's payment info and relays that to Notification System, and the Notification System will need to relay that payment information to the processor and to the ice cream maker if the payment is accepted. Once the ice cream maker is done with the ice cream, it sends a signal to check if the cone detector detected any cones. If there is a cone, then the scoop of ice cream drops onto the cone.

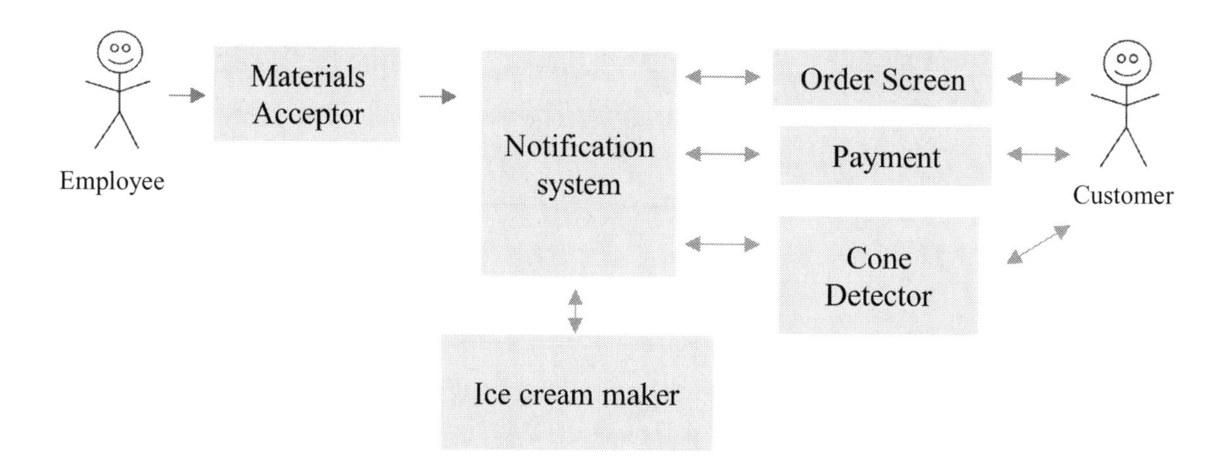

So, given what we know so far, we have drawn an AFD for the ice cream machine above. But I find the example with the ice cream machine to be simplistic, so let's find another example where it's little bit more complicated.

4.2.1 AFD More Complicated Example

So, imagine that you are designing a mobile application. Let's pick a platform: Apple iOS on the iPhones. This mobile application is similar to Instagram. The user takes pictures with the Instagram app, applies filters to the pictures, and shares it with her friends. The friends see the shared pictures on their Instagram app. Pretty simple application, right? How would you draw the AFD for this mobile app?

Step 1: Who are the Actors?
The primary actor(s) is the user. The secondary actor(s) are the friends.

Step 2: What are the modules?
Think what are the things that must happen in this app:

a. Photo taking
b. Photo filtering
c. Photo sharing
d. Photo viewing

There are 4 main tasks that this app does. The first 3 are performed by the user. The last tasks is done by the friends. Let's go deeper into each one.

a. What happens during the photo taking task? The photo is assumed to be captured by the camera and must reside in the app's memory, so there must be some space/storage or database on the device to hold this information. So, we now have a **"Photo Storage"** concept that we would need to incorporate into the diagram.
b. What happens in the photo filtering task? The photo is retrieved from the Photo Storage and a single filter can be applied to it. The new filtered picture is stored in the Photo Storage.
c. What happens in the photo sharing task? A photo a set of friends are identified for sharing. Where are the friends? They must exist in memory so there should be something to hold it; let's call this **"People database".** The people database is too big though, so we want to have something that will only give us the friends of a given person. So, there must exist another process that provides this info. Let's call this new process: **"Friends Finder".** Once the photo is "shared", the state of the photo may change and the friend's view of the mobile app will change too in order to show the new photo. For the state of the photo change, let's make this a subtask of photo sharing task. For the friend's view, that's the next step below.
d. What happens when the photo is set to be viewed? We need to create a new concept that allows friends to view all the photos that is being shared. This item is kind of like a queue and every person has a **"to be displayed" queue**. Photos get off the queue when the friend sees it and new items are added to the queue when they are shared. This guarantees that a person will see all the photos that is being shared with him.

So far we have added the following new concepts to our diagram: **"Photo Storage", "People database", "Friends Finder", "to be displayed" queue.**

Step 3: What are the Actor to Modules interactions?

In step 1, we identified two actors. Let's pick one to start with: the main user. The User uses the mobile app to take photos, apply filters, and shares it. So, the user must interact with those modules.

The other actor is the friend(s). The friend uses the mobile app and views photos that are shared with her. So, the friend interacts with only the photo viewing module.

Step 4: What are the Modules to Modules interactions?

As a recap, we have the following modules identified from Steps 1 and 2.

- Photo taking
- Photo filtering
- Photo sharing
- Photo viewing
- Photo Storage
- People database
- Friends Finder
- To be displayed queue.

Given what we have written in Step 2 about how we derived the new modules, I think we understand how the modules interact with each other.

Let's start diagraming!

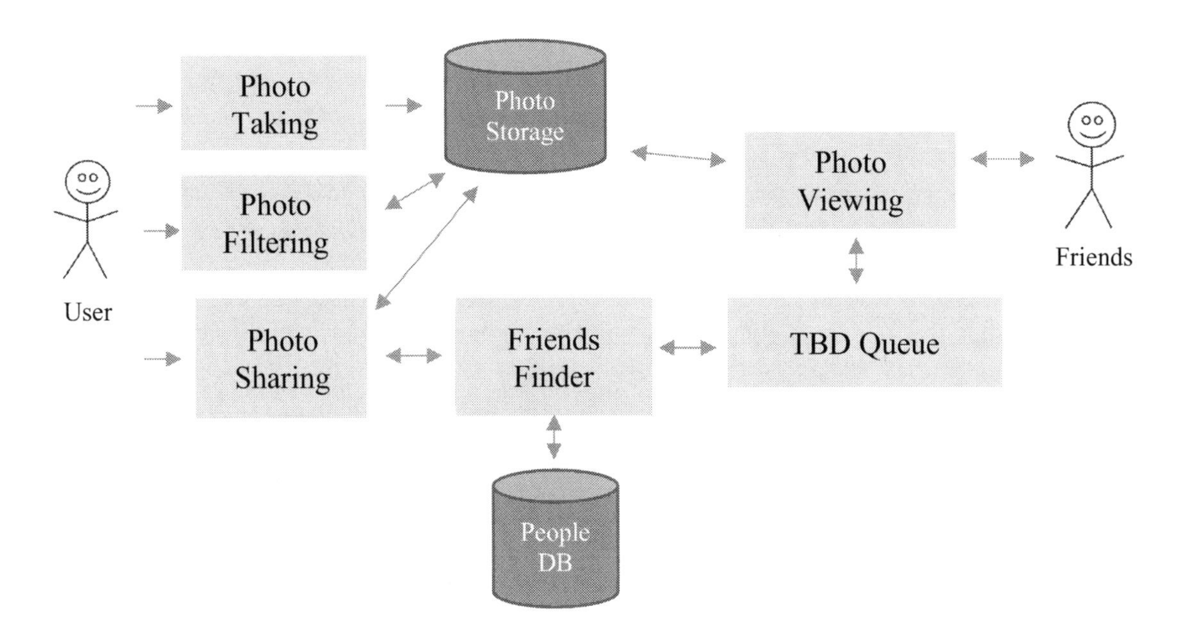

4.2.2 Commonly Asked Questions about AFD

Are there standard rules to draw the modules?

There is no set standard to draw the modules, but there are some guidelines in which you should follow.

- Modules are usually drawn with a rectangular box.
- Databases are drawn using the cylinder
- Computers, mobile devices, servers are drawn with their respective icons (i.e. show a computer, a mobile device, and server)
- People are drawn with either a stick figure or a simple diagram showing the head and body.

Do I need to diagram every single interaction?

No, you only want to diagram the important interactions. You don't want to pollute the diagrams with too many arrows, but you also don't want to leave out interactions that are non-obvious. So, it becomes a tradeoff of what to diagram and what not to diagram. If you are concerned, err on the side of over-diagraming than under-diagraming.

Should I show the "Internet" or other intermediary mediums?

This depends, but if the process is going over the Internet to make a call, it's important to draw that. Why? Because the call is external to the system and when things go outside the system, there are security and compliance issues that may arise. So, it's important to document that interaction so that the right folks can take a look further if needed.

The modules sound all like verbs? Is that always the case?

No. A module is a concept and a module must either do something (verb) or be something (noun). In the example, most of the modules did something as there was some action or operation associated with it. But there are other modules like the database that are not exactly verbs but are there to represent storage, as an example.

4.3 Sequence Diagrams

Finally, we have a third type of diagram that tells us "how parts of the system does it" over time. This diagram is called a sequence diagram. A sequence diagram shows the flow of calls from one actor (or module or class) to another. A call is invoking a method of function.

Sequence diagrams have time as one of the important dimensions, which is what the other two diagrams that we discussed above don't have as they are static diagrams. The other important dimension are the actors. Each vertical line, called lifelines, in a sequence diagram is an actor and is a participant in the sequence diagram. An actor could be a person, a system, or a module in a system. By connecting the actors via invoking each other's methods and returning the results of the invocation (if any), the sequence diagram looks like a zig-zag drawing.

Sequence Diagrams have:

- **Lifelines** – represents actors/participants in the diagram
- **Messages** (Calls or actions) – represents the synchronous or asynchronous calls from one lifeline to another
  - **Descriptions/Signatures** – each Message has a simple short phrase or actual API call signature for the call and return result
  - **Time** – represented by the angle of the message.
- **Loops** – represents any repeated logic
- **Comment** – verbiage next to the lifeline to document any notes in English

Another word we use for sequence diagrams are "dynamic diagrams" because they show how the system works in action. It's not static. Static diagrams are snapshots. They are a "moment in time". UML class diagrams and architecture diagrams (both layered and flow) are static diagrams. On the other hand, a sequence diagram is a dynamic diagram.

The diagram on the next page shows a sample of an interaction in the ICM. The diagram shows 2 actors: User and the ICM. The time dimension starts at the top and goes down with time. The first action is the User using the ICM and saying "I want one strawberry scoop on a sugar cone". ICM replies with the price. User provides the money. Finally, ICM provides the order.

Although the example provided is simplistic, you can imagine very complicated cases that have more than one actor. In fact, the example showed us an example of a "black box" sequence diagram of the ICM because we don't get to see what's going on inside the ICM, we just know it takes orders and accepts money. You should start out each system that you are trying to understand with the black box method.

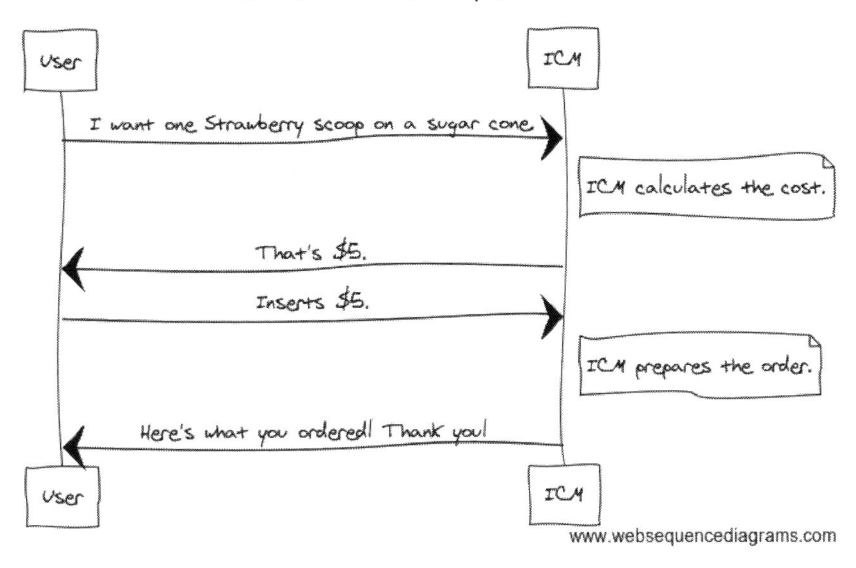

Now, let's dive a little deeper into what this ICM black box looks like inside. Below is another diagram that expands on the diagram above. Notice how many actors we have in the system now. Notice what those actors are. (I've changed the name of the modules to be "Order Processor", "Cost Calculator", and "Dispenser" to make it more aligned with the previous sequence diagram).

Notice the flow of calls that happen. We have broken down "ICM" into three different modules. In the diagram, I used words to describe the calls from one actor to another. More formally though, you should use the actual API call method if possible. Using phrases and verbiage to describe the call is fine, but you also want to let other engineers know the actual call method so that it can be referenced later if needed.

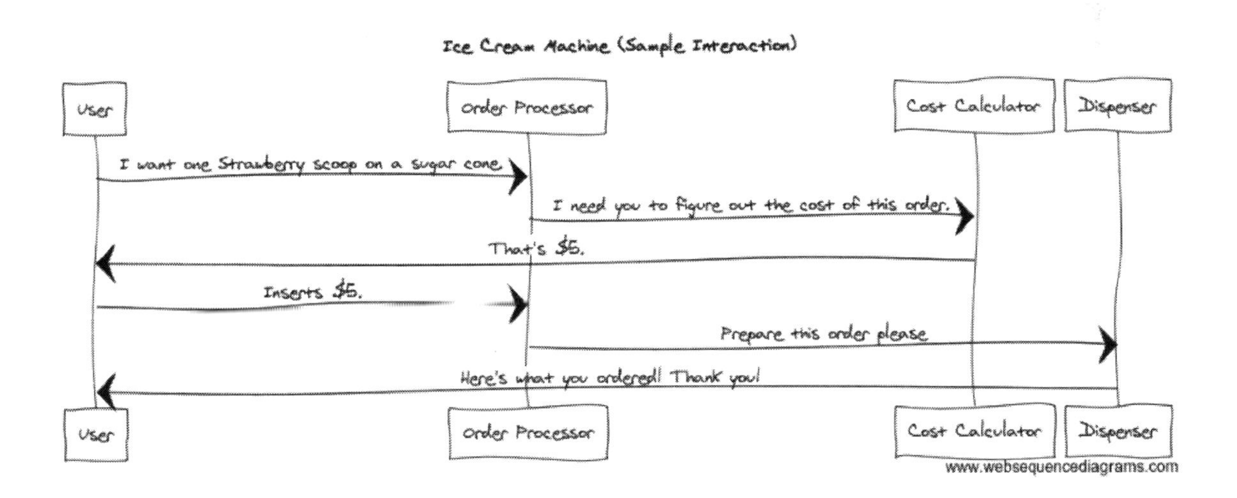

Exercise: Given the architecture diagrams that we last drew, how would you translate that into a sequence diagram?

4.3.1 Formal Sequence Diagrams

On the previous page, we saw casual sequence diagrams. Casual sequence diagrams had only one type of lifeline, one type of message, and comments. We use casual sequence diagrams in, you guessed it, in casual settings like on a whiteboard or when we are drawing out an idea very quickly. But if you wanted to be (more) formal, UML provides a formal approach to diagraming sequence diagrams. Let's formalize everything that we've learned about sequence diagrams.

4.3.1.1 Lifelines

There exists five different types of lifelines:

- Actor
- Boundary
- Control
- Entity
- Object

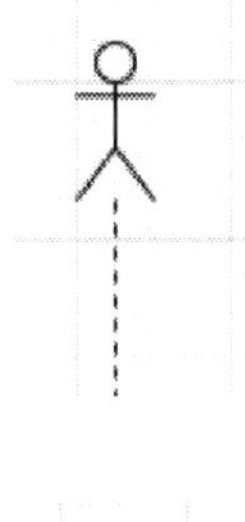

An **Actor** lifeline is used when a human participant is involved.

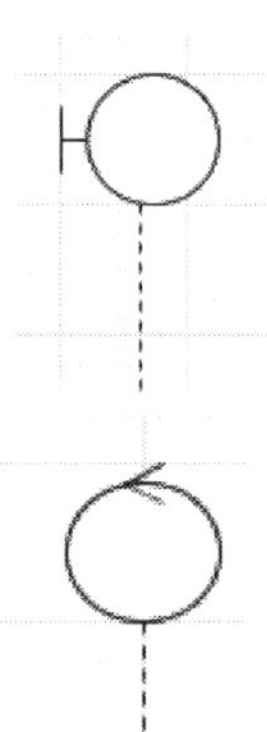

A **Boundary** lifeline is used when you want to show a system boundary such as a user interface, networking elements (i.e. Internet), databases.

A **Control** lifeline is used to signify a controller entity. This can be the entity or concept that manages, coordinates the various activities between the modules or other entities.

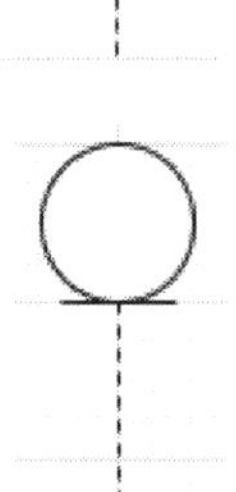

An **Entity** lifeline is used to signify the entity that manages the data. "Book" concept would be considered an Entity lifeline because the Book keeps track of all the data belonging to Book.

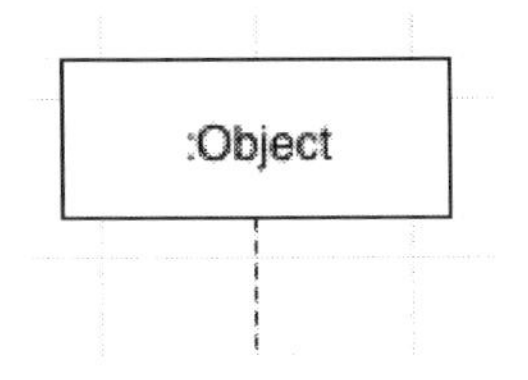

An **Object** lifeline is used to signify an instantiation of the class. Almost all your lifelines will be this type of lifeline.

4.3.1.2 Activation of Lifeline

Lifelines by itself are inactive by default. You can't make a call to a dotted lifeline; it needs to be activated! The way that we specify activation is with a long narrow rectangular bar. The official terminology is "activation bar", or some just call it the candlestick. (If you call it the candlestick then the dotted line is called the "wick", just like a candle's wick.)

The length of the candlestick specifies how long the object is active for. If it does a long process like a computation or a computation that depends on other computation, then the length will be long. You don't necessarily need to specify the length of time, but you could if you want to in the comment.

The diagram below shows one object being active two separate times. One with a short candlestick to signify a short active time and one with a longer candlestick to signify a longer active time.

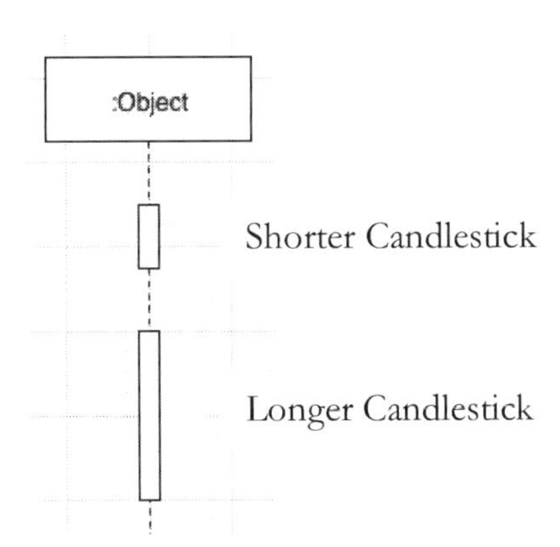

4.3.1.3 Messages

Messages are the calls that one lifeline makes to another. They are basically method or operation calls. A message has the following elements.

- Constructive or Destructive
- Asynchronous or Synchronous
- Message description
- Time

Constructive or Destructive

All messages are constructive unless they destroy the object (destructive). When a message is called from one lifeline to another, the lifeline of the callee becomes active if it is not active already; we say that this type of message is constructive. When a message is called from one lifeline to another, the lifeline of the callee becomes de-active; we say that this type of message is destructive.

We use the letter "X" at the end of the dotted line to denote that a lifeline has ended.

Asynchronous or Synchronous

A message can either be asynchronous or synchronous. A synchronous call blocks the process until the call completes. An asynchronous call is non-blocking and therefore does not need to wait for the call to complete.

If you ask your friend to grab a cup of coffee, you should wait for her reply before you start heading out to the coffee shop. We call that request synchronous.

If you decide you are going to go get coffee anyway but you wouldn't mind a friend to go with you, you can ask your friend but start heading out regardless of her response. We call that request asynchronous.

The diagram below shows an example synchronous request to Object A, then an asynchronous request to Object B, then a destructive message to Object A.

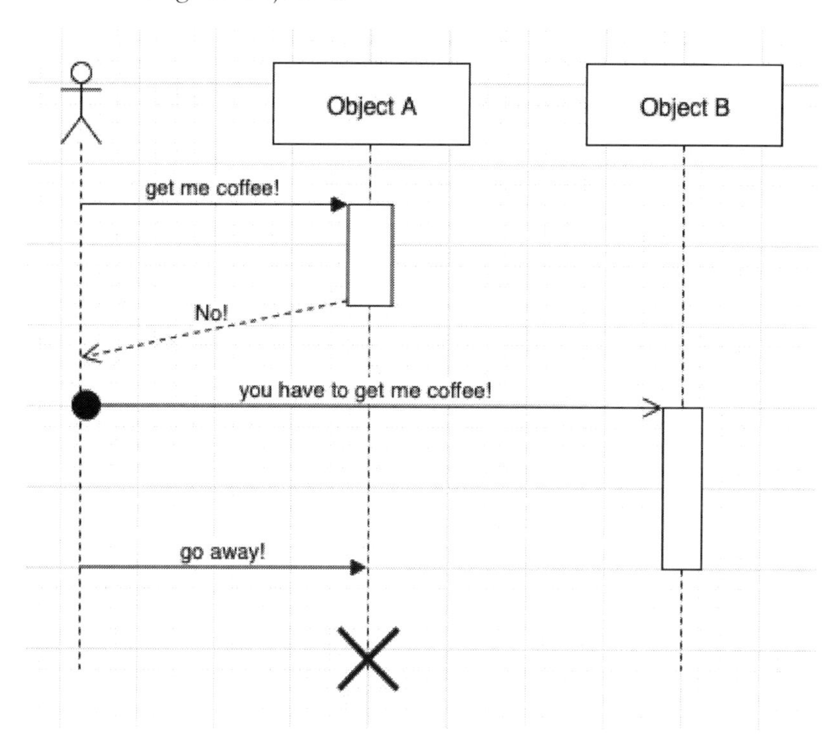

Message Description

The text that goes along with the message describes the context of the message. "Get me Coffee!" in the diagram above is an example of a message description. You can use English or you can be more formal.

The formality stems from the fact that a message is a method call and therefore a method signature is the best way to represent. The signature has four components: a message_name, which is the method name, parameters, which is the arguments that the method accepts, return type, which is the type of the value to be returned, and finally the attribute, which is the attribute name in the object. Although this is formal, none of the components are actually required.

```
attribute = message_name (parameters): return type
```

Time

The text that goes along with the message describes the context of the message. The message labelled "Get me Coffee!" in the example below is slanted to signify that time (although unspecified) is required to initiate the call from one lifeline to another.

The Time dimension is always the down direction and to the right. So, it's entirely optional to show a slanted line to indicate time. Instead, you can replicate the second example labelled "you have to get me coffee!" by placing a time indicator in the box to indicate the length of time it would take for the call.

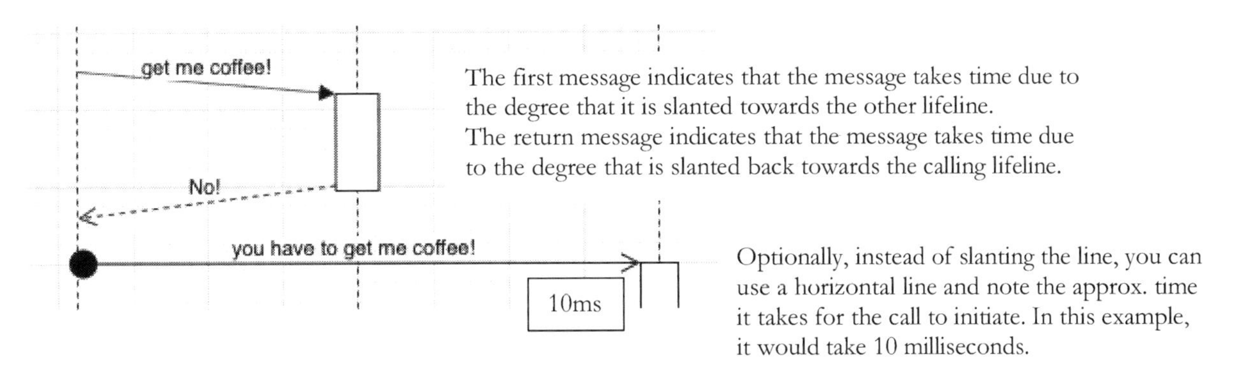

get me coffee!
No!
you have to get me coffee!
10ms
The first message indicates that the message takes time due to the degree that it is slanted towards the other lifeline.
The return message indicates that the message takes time due to the degree that is slanted back towards the calling lifeline.
Optionally, instead of slanting the line, you can use a horizontal line and note the approx. time it takes for the call to initiate. In this example, it would take 10 milliseconds.

4.3.1.4 Loops

The Loop is a box around a set of messages that indicate that there is some logic that is segmented from the rest. In this particular example below, the loop specifies a logic of the user asking Object C a question and waiting for a result, repeatedly. The back and forth continues until either the result is satisfactory to the user or based on a certain number of times; notice how the logic to end the loop is not shown in the UML sequence diagram. Instead, you can use Comments to show the logic, if needed.

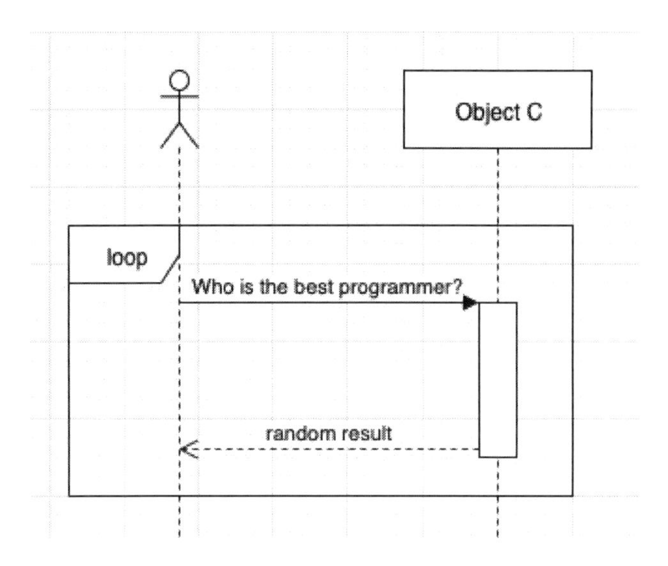

4.3.1.5 Comments

A comment is a note shown next to some logic or concept in the diagram. In the example below, we show a comment about the loop's end logic and placed the comment next to the loop so that it is clear that it belongs to the loop. You can also draw a line from the comment box to the loop for clarity.

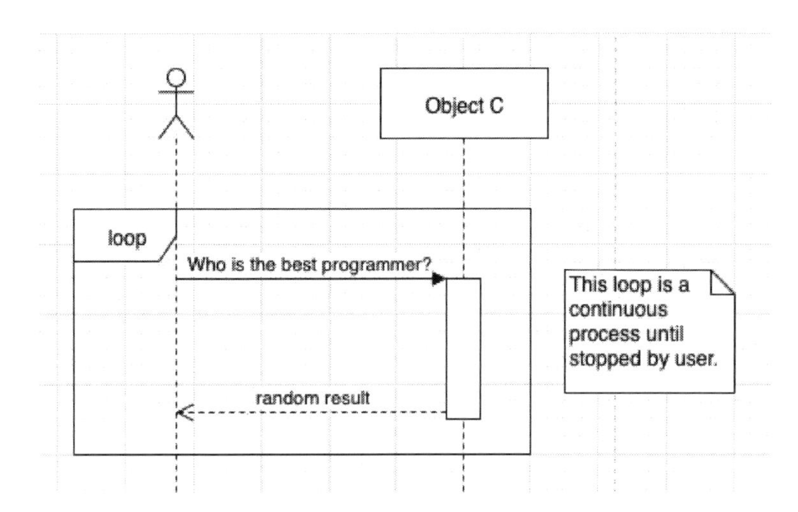

4.3.1.6 Example

What does the following UML sequence diagram do?

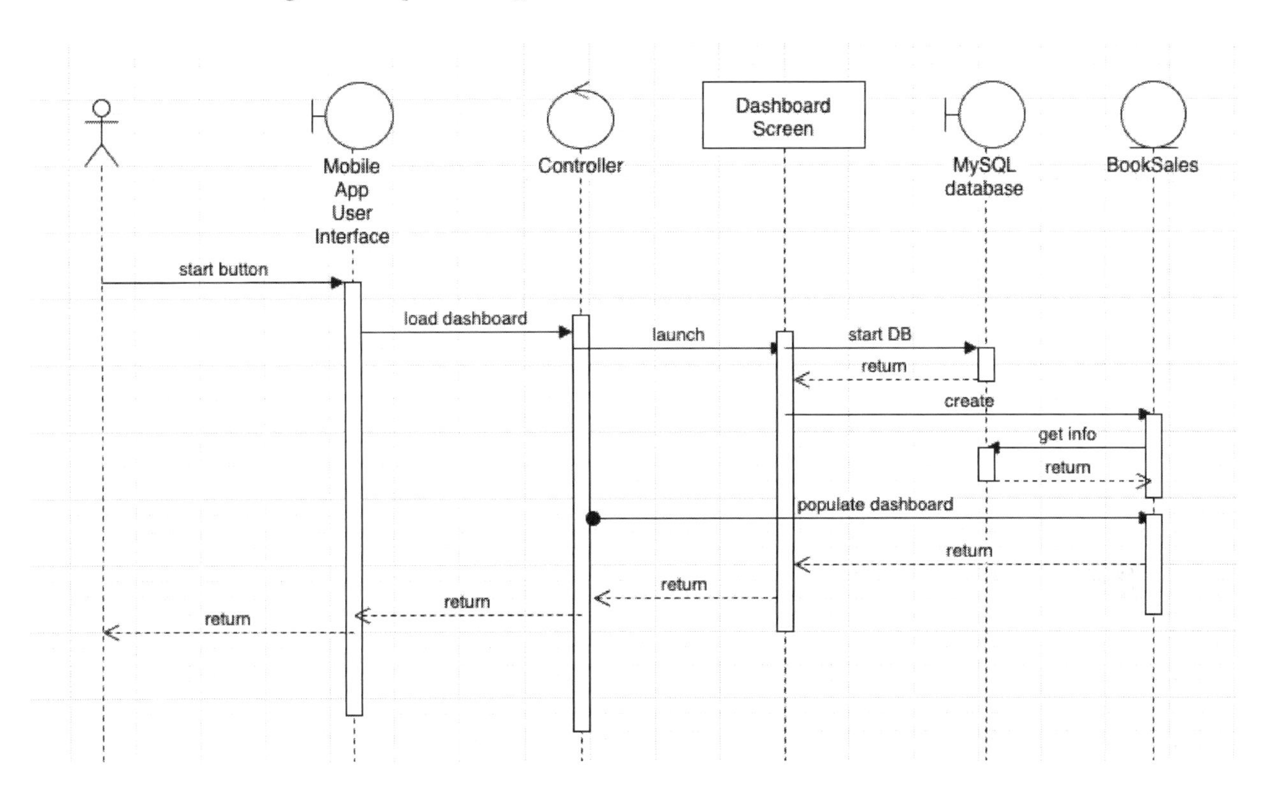

We first start from the left to the right. We see an actor lifeline and the first message is a "start button" action from the user to a mobile interface. This action seems to launch a cascade of other calls – first to the controller to orchestrate the call to the dashboard, which starts the database. The dashboard screen logic asks the BookSales entity to get some information so that the dashboard can be populated with its data. Although the end result is not given, we assume that the user sees a dashboard with information about BookSales.

4.3.2 Commonly Asked Questions about Sequence Diagrams

When should I use casual vs formal sequence diagrams?
For documents like a Design Spec, use formal sequence diagrams whenever possible or when there is a strict procedure to clearly and articulately document the various interactions. Otherwise, a casual sequence diagram is fine for most purposes. The goal is ultimately to get your idea across.

How should I select which use case or sub-system to diagram?
You want to select a sub-use case or sub-system that follows the following guidelines:

- Show an overview
  - For this type of diagram, detail is not what matters, it's about knowing the participants in the system.
- Show a sub-use case
  - Focus on one single sub-use case that does one single task. If you decide to pick or combine multiple use cases, your diagram may not end up being clear or may be too long to digest. Example: Show how a user turns on the TV is one sequence diagram. Showing how a user turns off the TV is another sequence diagram. (You can technically combine these two due to their simplicity, but as a general rule, not all use cases are that simple).
- Show a sub-system
  - Focus on that one single task that that sub-system does, but don't lose sight of the specific sub-use case.
    Example: When a user turns on the TV, show the behind the scenes details of the objects/modules involved.

How much detail should I put in a sequence diagram?

For a formal sequence diagram, place as much detail as you can that is non-obvious. But you don't want to pollute the diagram either. The best thing you can do is pick one specific use case or sub-use case and diagram that. You never want to diagram the entire use case if that use case is deemed to be large. In the example in the previous section, we diagramed one sub use case, which is the launching the mobile app use case and what the user first sees.

You will also want to be as accurate as possible especially if you are to use message descriptions; use the exact method call whenever possible.

You will want the timing and ordering to be as accurate as possible because if you diagram something that is out of order, then that is not how the system works and you will have drawn an incorrect diagram.

Do I depict the entire system in one sequence diagram?

No. You should almost never do this, unless the entire system is super simple. The goal of the sequence diagram is to elicit and illustrate how one part of the system works, not the entire system. Focus on that one part because of its non-obviousness or dependencies with other systems. Keep the sequence diagram to one page or half page if possible, although this is not a hard rule.

4.4 Tools

There are many software tools to diagram architectures and sequence diagrams. But before embarking on that journey, you should always use a pen/pencil to prepare. I've included a list of commonly used tools. By no means am I endorsing any of the tools listed, they only serve as educational purposes for the reader.

Tools to draw Architecture Diagrams:

Many programs exist, here are some recommendations:

- Paper and pencil
- Microsoft Visio
- Microsoft PowerPoint
- Microsoft Word
- A whiteboard

Tools to draw Sequence Diagrams:

Many programs exist, here are some recommendations:

- Paper and pencil
- http://www.websequencediagrams.com
- http://draw.io
- Microsoft Visio
- Microsoft PowerPoint
- A whiteboard

[This page left intentionally blank]

4.5 Exercises

1. Use your favorite search engine to find the architecture layer diagram of the Linux operating system.
    a. Which modules interface with the hardware directly?
    b. Identify the Linux Kernel.
    c. Where are the applications?

2. What is the difference between an architecture layer and architecture flow diagram?

3. What is a static vs dynamic diagram? Provide examples.

4. Restaurant Order App

    a. Background: In-n-Out Now, a fast food burger joint has decided to offer the capability of ordering your meal via a mobile app and then pick up through a separate drive through lane. A user downloads and installs the "In-n-Out Now" orders hamburgers, cheeseburgers, or fries, and pays in the mobile app, and submits the order.

    b. Draw the AFD of this mobile app.

    c. Draw the ALD of this mobile app.

    d. Draw the sequence diagram.

5. Sprinkler System

    a. Imagine you had a home sprinkler system that controls watering the lawn and plants in your yard. What would an architecture layer diagram for this system look like?

    b. Imagine you had a home sprinkler system that controls watering the lawn and plants in your yard. What would an architecture flow diagram for this system look like?

    c. Draw sequence diagrams of the interaction between the user and the system. Show how the user wants to configure the system by
    (1) setting up the system,
    (2) configuring a set date and time to turn on the water
    (3) turning the system off.

    You'll have to make assumptions and "design" what you think the system should do and not do. To tackle this problem, best thing to start out with is to write your own simple casual use cases.

[This page left intentionally blank]

5 DESIGN SPECIFICATION

The Design Specification or Software Functional Specification is a document that details how the system under implementation is designed. It is a document, written by the engineers, that specifies how the engineers will satisfy the product requirements. The "Design Spec" document serves the purpose of documenting the design – where we have translated our analysis into design.

Our goal as software engineers is to make sure we develop software that satisfies the requirements of the user. If we accomplish this, our job is done. As software engineers, we have two main and highly important deliverables: Design Spec and code.

[The Design Spec] is our
main non-coding deliverable
as engineers

This chapter is about the Design Spec. It includes, but not limited to, the three types of UML diagrams that we have learned so far: Class Diagram, Architecture, and Sequence Diagrams. The diagrams, in addition to the verbiage that we engineers would have to write, serve as the main parts of the Design Specification. It is our main non-coding deliverable as engineers.

In this chapter, we will take the Ice Cream Machine example that we have been working on and create a sample Design Spec.

Fair warning: Because we haven't covered all the topics yet, you will need to take the UML diagrams that you see at face value. So, we will assume that you have created the UML diagrams that you will see in the next sections. In the next chapter, we will learn how to translate from use case requirements to UML. The reason for this ordering is that you understand at a high level what needs to be done, instead of going to deep and losing sight of the big picture.

Terminology: Design Specification is one of many different words used to describe the design document that the engineers create to layout their system design. Other names are "Software Functional Specification", "Software Design Specification", "Technical Software Requirements", and more. Regardless of what you call it, the ideas for each of those concepts are the same. To add to this confusion, in this book, we will exclusively use "Design Spec" as short hand for "Design Specification".

5.1 Contents of Design Spec

The contents of a Design Spec largely depends on what company you work for. At the company, there is usually a set template that is defined by a committee within the company and has been approved by legal and compliance departments of the company so that the company can satisfy certain governmental or non-governmental rules and regulations. However, there are five things that all Design Specs should have. Let's provide an overview and the subsequent sections will dive deeper into each.
Five things all Design Specs should minimally have:

- Introduction
- System Overview and Design Considerations
- Architecture and System design
- Sub-system or Feature Design
- Glossary

5.1.1 Introduction

The introduction describes a summarization of the purpose of the document and the system. The goal is that for anyone new to the team, he or she can read the introduction and get an idea of what the project is about. This section should contain an Executive Summary, for the executives and for those short on time. It's actually for the author as well because if you can distill your thoughts into a concise summary using terminology that anyone can understand without being overly complicated or buzzword heavy, then it shows you understand what you are designing. The approximate length of this section is about a page long, with some going over a few pages for more complex projects.

5.1.2 System Overview

Once the introduction has been written, we are getting closer to the meat of the project. In this critical section, we want to list what will be built, what the project scope is, list the high-level features, list and discuss the conventions used, and finally list any constraints, risks, dependencies, and assumptions.

What will be built

List or replicate the requirements in PRD by reference number (i.e. REQ-NNNN) and state whether it is satisfied or not satisfied. This is critical because although a PRD might state that REQ-0123 is HIGH priority, the design may not be satisfied for a myriad of reasons given by the engineering team. Usually, the

Product Manager will be informed of the investigation and decision so that there is no surprises on either teams, and that a workaround or collaborative effort to decide how to address the missing requirement would be at least investigated or in the worst case dropped from the requirements as not essential. Here's an example:

Product Requirement Number	Engineering Assessment
REQ-001	Satisfied
REQ-002	Not Satisfied – Requirement infeasible
REQ-003	Not satisfied – workaround exists.
REQ-004	Satisfied

Project Scope

The description of the scope of the project is essential as well. It's similar to "What will be built" but fine tunes it a bit by either (a) increasing the scope of the project so that a more general approach and general solution is being built, (b) decreasing the scope of the project so that a certain timeline or focus can be met, or (c) stating that the specified scope in the PRD is the plan of record.

In (a), this case exists because far too often we build specifically for a solution and then a few months later the customer(s) want a more general solution that does many more things. So, the engineers have to go back and retrofit the old code to make it work with the more general solution. This is akin to the idiomatic saying "missing the forest for the trees".

In (b), this case exists because also far too often we have grander ambitions than what can actually be done in the allotted time. All projects have a deadline that was calculated by someone for a reason, so in order to meet that deadline, certain features or items would need to be cut or massaged to still meet the most basic requirements.

Finally, in (c), this (gets better with time) case is when both teams – product management and engineering – are on the same page and so everything written is perfect and ideal factoring in the work required and resourcing. This case is for the experienced.

List of High Level Features

The "What is in" section covers this from a PRD mapping perspective, but from a high-level perspective, we want to also summarize what's in via a list of feature descriptions. As an example:

Feature	Engineering Assessment
Collect user data via an API to Facebook's advertising database	In
Collect user data via an API to Google's advertising database	Out
Module that generates the top 10 advertising campaigns	In
Module that allows users to set a deadline for an ad placement.	In

Conventions

Conventions are specific notation or design principles that the engineer has decided to use that may not be standard or not known by many. If that is the case, then the engineer is obliged to inform others what convention(s) s/he has decided to use.

Example: In this Design Spec, the author uses the symbol "+" to mean multiplicity of 0 to many, instead of "*".

Constraints, risks, dependencies, and assumptions

This is the section that most experienced people will be looking at almost all the time. As the engineer, you need to be realistic with what you design and sometimes because no code has been written you might not know what to expect, especially if you rely on other teams or external teams. So, we list any inkling or anything that could go wrong with the project in this section.

Here are some sample risks:

Risks	**Impact**
The system may not immediately turn on when the user presses the "On" button.	User may continue to press the "On" button until the system turns on, but may inadvertently break the button from pressing too many times.
The ice cream may melt inside the machine if we not regulate the temperature inside.	We will need to build a refrigerator inside the ice cream machine in order to keep the ice cream cold.
The scoop of ice cream may not drop directly on the cone and so might fall on the floor.	Employee will need to clean up the mess and place another order. Customer will get mad.

Here are some sample dependencies:

Dependencies	**Impact**
The hardware mechanism that detects the cone does not exist in the current market.	We suggest building this component ourselves or work with the vendor to build for us.
We need UL certification for the power that the machine will need.	Get tested by Underwriter's Laboratory.
The team that will provide the ice cream making software is all on vacation!	Contemplate how this situation is even possible, but regardless, ask them to send us a postcard.

5.1.3 Architecture and System Design

This important section provides an overview of the entire system under development. This means that some of the key parts of the section is the overall system architecture layer and flow diagrams, overall UML class diagram (if exists), and a high-level sequence diagram going over the top main use cases. The idea is to help the reader understand at a high level your design, without going into details about any features. Instead, the details about the features belongs in the next section.

Recall our architecture layer diagram for the Ice Cream Machine (ICM) below. The Architecture overview section is the perfect place this diagram. In addition to the diagram, you'll want to explain in words the diagram and why you have chosen to design it the way it is designed. You'll want to discuss any nuances in the design that is not apparent or esoteric.

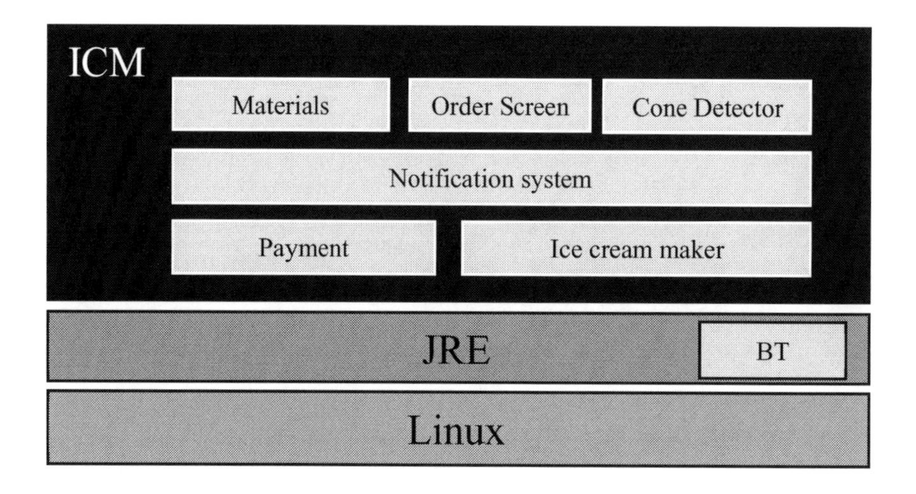

Once you have the architecture diagrams, you'll want to include a sequence diagram. See below for a rendition of a sequence diagram to include the 6 modules that we drew.

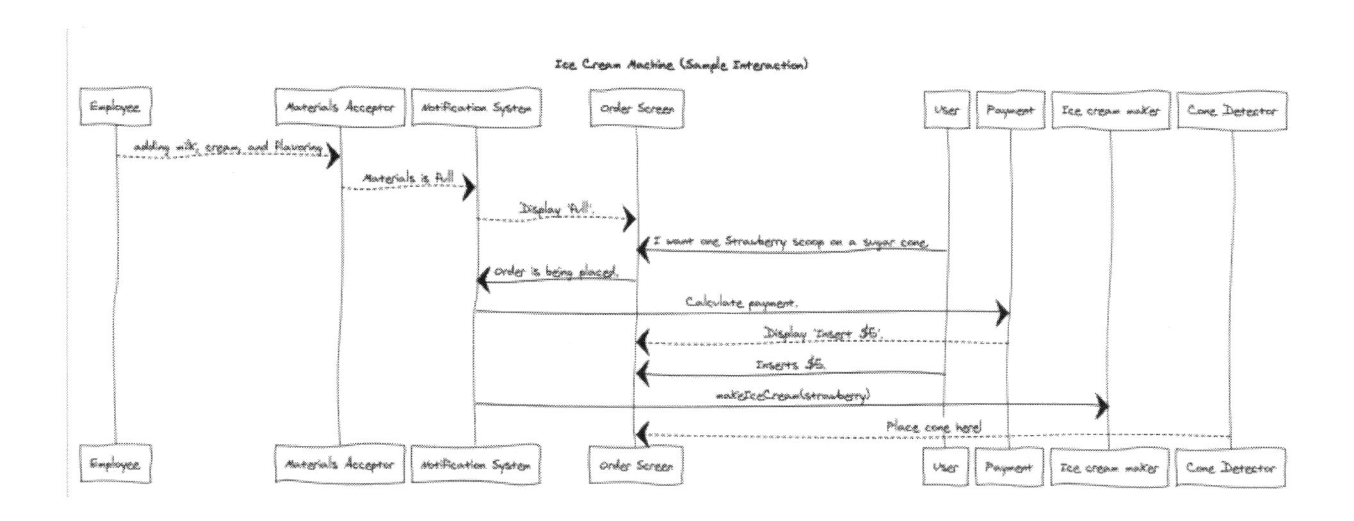

Notice the two main people actors: Employee and User. Also notice that not all interactions are drawn. There are many other details that can be included. For example, the payment flow can be extended into many more interactions between the User and the ICM machine. But as an overall sequence diagram for our Design Spec, it is "almost" sufficient for our needs. (As an exercise, you can add the following missing interactions in the diagram to "complete" it:

(1) Employee places the cone,
(2) the scoop of ice cream drops on the cone,
(3) the employee takes the cone and gives it to the user/customer.)

So far, we've included two diagrams. Should we need to add a UML Class Diagram? Not necessarily, but you can. Since the ICM is a relatively straightforward project, let's include the UML class diagram in this section.

Note: We have not yet learned to convert use cases and requirements to UML class diagrams. We learn this in the next chapter.

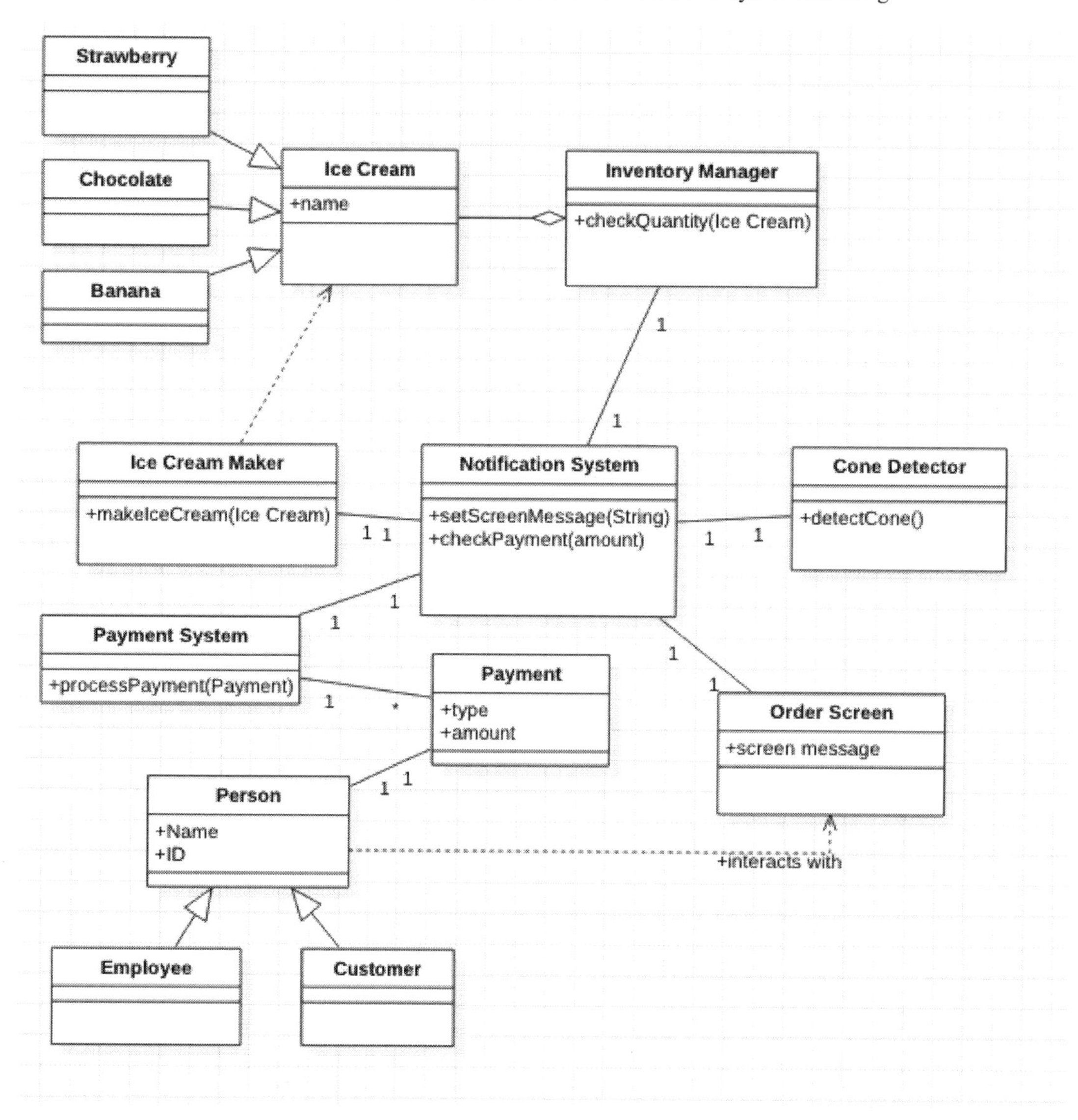

So, we now have all three of the diagrams that we have learned so far! In the next chapter, we'll learn how to create the ICM UML class diagram. But first, let's finish off the two remaining sections of the Design Spec.

5.1.4 Sub-System and Feature Design

The sub-system and feature design are exactly what it says it is. We want to expound on each of the modules that we laid out in the architecture diagram and we want to make it so clear that anyone who did not have any prior knowledge of the system can pick up our Design Spec and start coding immediately. That is our metric for success!

Before we begin, what are the features that we are required to build? The short PRD that we had to work with didn't say. So, let's make some assumptions in the absence of direction:

a) ICM takes materials as input
b) ICM takes human input such as order and payments
c) ICM makes ice cream given the inputs
d) ICM places scoop of ice cream on cone

At the crux of it, ICM only does those 4 things. Yes, it may do other things such as give error messages and things like that, but the core functionality are those four things. Those are the features that we need to design. Each feature is really a sub-system because each one can be independently built from another although they do have some interactions with each other.

What about the six modules we drew in the Architecture layer diagram? How do they relate to those four features listed above? Recall the six modules: Materials Acceptor, Order Screen, Notification System, Cone detector, Payment, and Ice cream maker.

The six modules actually map to the four features. See table below. Notification system spans across all 4 features and feature (B) consists of two modules.

FEATURE	MODULE MAPPING	
A) ICM TAKES MATERIALS AS INPUT	Materials Acceptor	
B) ICM TAKES HUMAN INPUT SUCH AS ORDER AND PAYMENTS	Order Screen, Payment	Notification System
C) ICM MAKES ICE CREAM GIVEN THE INPUTS	Ice cream maker	
D) ICM PLACES SCOOP OF ICE CREAM ON CONE	Cone detector	

Is our Architecture diagram wrong because we have a mismatch (i.e. not a 1-to-1 mapping) of features and modules? Not at all. A feature may be accomplished with one or more modules. Features are a higher-level construct that external people to the project such as customers, users, business people use to refer to what the system does. Modules are a lower level construct used to help engineers map features to what needs to be built. So, in most cases, there is not going to be a 1-to-1 mapping.
Let's pick 2 of the features and do a sample sub-system design.

5.1.4.1 Sample Feature #1 – (A) ICM takes materials as input

Before we begin, we must understand what this feature needs to accomplish; we need to satisfy the requirements. Where do we get the use cases and requirements? The PRD. Because the PRD was missing important minute details, it's up to us to work with the Product Manager and level down (sometimes level up) the conversation from business requirements to technical requirements. Let's assume we have done that and we have the below information from the Product Manager, which we all agree are the problems we wish to solve.

- **Use Case:** ICM machines takes in 3 flavors of raw materials into individualized containers that store the materials. The user is able to check, via the ICM machine screen, how much material is left so that she can add more material when needed. The screen will tell her a specific percentage, one for each of the 3 flavors, ranging from 0% (empty) to 100% (full) in whole number percentages.
- **Input:** The device takes raw materials as input. The container holding the raw materials will have something that detects how much raw materials is left so that the user is aware. This information will be accessible on the order screen (but only visible by the employee).
- **Output**: Information about how much raw material is left on a per container basis. Since there are 3 containers, one for each flavor, there should be three outputs. The output number should be a percentage ranging from 0 to 100%.
- **Software**: As we are not responsible for the hardware aspects (i.e. the container, the sensor, etc.), we focus on the software system. This particular system sounds like a detector of raw material to see how much is left and reports it to another system when asked.

The system looks pretty simple because all it does is one single function. Let's dig a little deeper into the actual method calls. Since we know there are 3 flavors, we need to have a method to get the remaining level given one or more of the flavors. We envision this in code as this: int getRemainingLevel(IceCream ic). This method returns an integer, which would be the percentage left of the given flavor as input. We could also have many variants of this method, for example, one that accepts no parameters and returns all three percentages. But let's assume we have chosen the one that we designed and go with that.

Great! We now have a method! Do we need any other methods? I don't think so, at least given the output above, only one is required for now. What about attributes? There doesn't appear to be any because there are no properties that are specific to this module.

So far so good. We have a method and no attributes. What do we call this module? We can call it the Materials Acceptor, but that name doesn't really represent what it does. It's a software module, not a hardware module so we need to give it a software-ish name. How about Inventory Manager?

Hmm… where did we see Inventory Manager before? In the UML class diagram in the architecture section! It is there! But in the diagram we had a different method name: checkQuantity(Ice Cream). So, we need to pick one (checkQuantity or getRemainingLevel) and move on! Remember to make both diagrams consistent!

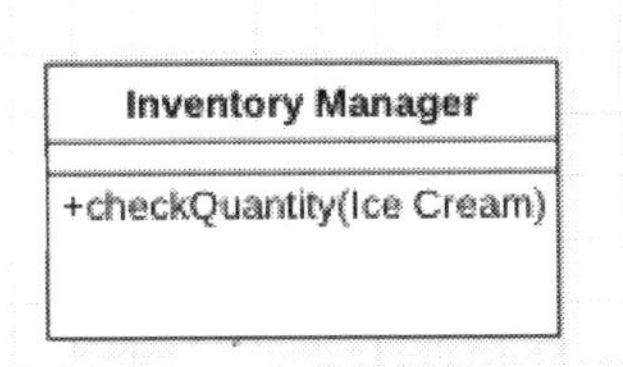

So, the solution to (A) is a class called Inventory Manager. Are we complete? Not quite, we haven't talked about the Ice Cream class yet, which the method accepts. Let's make sure we define and document that as well.

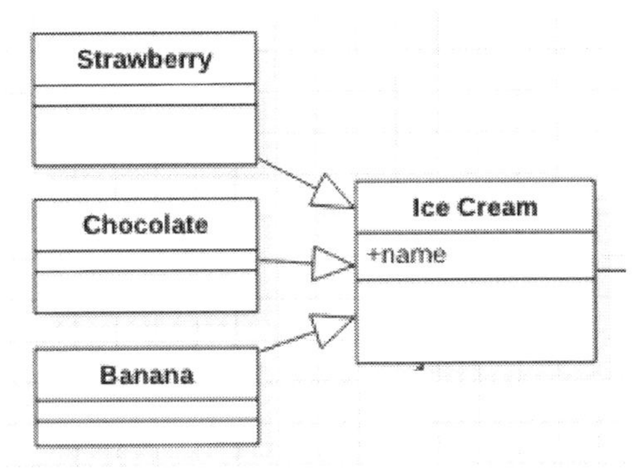

Ice Cream class has only one attribute, its name. We can use an ID or some type of identifier, but we have chosen a name instead. In this diagram we state that Ice Cream is the super class of Strawberry, Chocolate, and Banana classes or they inherit from the Ice Cream class.

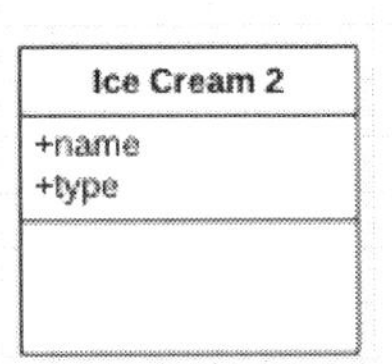

We chose to create a class for each type of Ice Cream. Why did we do that? Do we have to do it that way? Nope, here's another way to do it without having to create 3 additional classes, one for each flavor. Instead, we can embed the flavor in the "type" attribute. So, for strawberry flavor, we would say "type = 'Strawberry'" and so on. There are reasons why we choose one or the other, which is detailed on the next page.

Class or Attribute? How do you know?

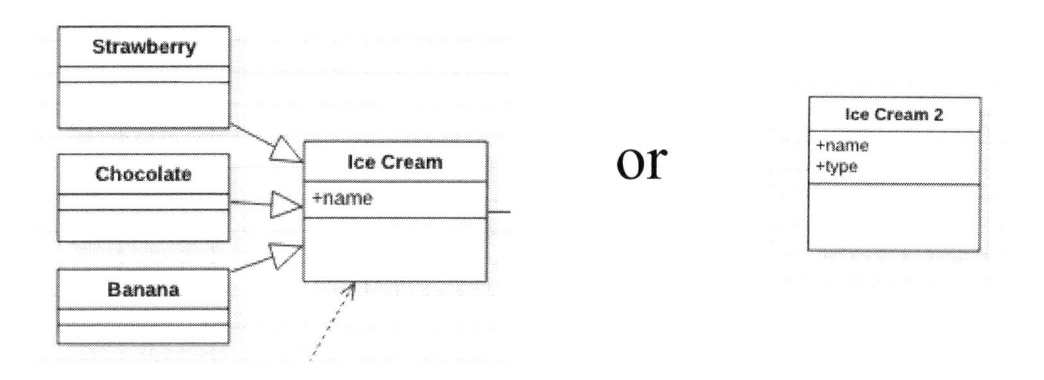

	PROs	CONs
Make them classes!	• Pure object oriented. Everything is an object.	• Lots of classes. • Potentially lots of type-casting in the code
Make them attributes!	• Potentially less code.	• Can't extend the subclasses. • Lots of code to refactor if you do decide to extend.

Answer: It depends. The true answer depends on how object oriented and how extensible you desire your code to be. Arguments for the class route say it's pure OO, while arguments for the attribute route say "that's a lot of classes to create!". No matter which side you are on, go through the pros and cons so that you can make an educated decision.

5.1.4.2 Sample Feature #2 – (B) ICM takes human input such as order and payments

Just like in the previous section, before we begin, we must understand what this feature needs to accomplish; we need to satisfy the requirements. Because the PRD was missing important minute details, it's up to us to work with the Product Manager and discuss the business and technical requirements. Let's assume we have done that and we have the below information from the Product Manager, which we all agree are the problems we wish to solve.

The newly modified use case (what the PRD should have said) is the following.

> *Customer looks at ICM and sees the screen say "Select a Flavor then press Order". Customer selects a flavor, sees it confirmed on the screen, and then presses the order button to confirm the order. He is then prompted to pay with a credit card. After he inserts the credit card, it processes the payment and he takes his card back. Screen will then display "Making Ice Cream!"*

- **Input:** This feature takes multiple inputs. Let's list them.
    - **#1 –** Human input
        - Button(s) to order. There are 4 buttons. Three buttons for each of the flavors and one button "Order" to place the order. There is no "Cancel" button.
        - Payment steps – User will be prompted to pay the amount displayed. The ICM machine will accept credit cards as the only form of payment so the user inputs this into the machine for processing.
    - #2 – Payment input
        - Credit Card only – The credit card is inserted into the machine for processing.
- **Output**: This feature also appears to output various items.
    - **#1** – Screen output
        - **Success or Failure of order**?
        - **Order confirmation**?
        - **Pricing**?
        - **Payment confirmation**?
- **Software**: As we are not responsible for the hardware aspects (i.e. the screen, the credit card slot), we focus on the software system. This particular system is multi-component and multi-function so there is a lot going on compared to the previous example.

  Let's decide to work on this in chronological order – following the use case step by step. The first thing the customer sees is the screen. Yes, this would be a Graphical User Interface (GUI) to the customer, but we are not modelling the GUI. Instead, we want to model the software system that the GUI interfaces with beneath. We want to make sure the system we design can accept the buttons, the payments, and alert the user as needed.

  The screen must have a display component that displays whatever messages that you tell it to. Let's create a method that allows us to do that: void setDisplayMessage(String). We can set this message to anything we desire and the screen would display this. The screen is going to be a class because we need a concept to hold items related to what gets displayed on the screen.

Next, let's do the buttons. Three buttons have very similar function so essentially this can be a method that takes as parameter the flavor of the ice cream. (This can also be three methods, but let's simplify). Let's call this method: void selectFlavor(Ice Cream). Once one of the flavor buttons is pressed, the setDisplayMessage(String) method in the Screen class is called prompting the customer to press the order button. The order button that has a different function than the flavor buttons, so that is another method. Let's call this method: boolean order().

Next, the customer gets prompted to pay, which is another setDisplayMessage method call. The customer inserts the credit card into the machine. The screen displays "Processing Credit Card" while processing and "Please take credit card" when it's done processing. When the credit card is taken back, the screen displays the final message. The last few steps are all setDisplayMessage calls except for the payment calls.

The payment calls are a bit tricky. It's not the screen processing the payment because the screen's job is only to display information. It's also not the buttons because the button's job are to set the flavor and confirm the order. So, there must exist another class that should handle the payments. Let's call this class "Payment System". Payment System's responsibility is to handle all payment related items and there appears to be only one method to do this that we would need to create: boolean processPayment (Payment). This method would take as parameter a form of payment and returns true if the payment has been processed or false if there was an error. We said that the form of payment was only going to be credit cards, so Payment should always equal credit cards. Payment should be a separate class that holds the information to be processed such as the amount to be charged, credit card number, expiration date, name, etc. To summarize, Payment System's job is to process, while Payment's job is to store (temporary) for processing.

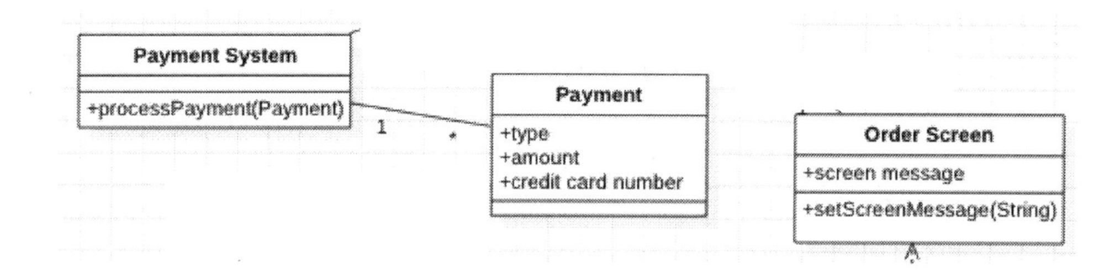

What about all the error scenarios? They would need to be handled by the logic in the methods itself and don't appear in the UML diagrams.

Notice that there is no association between Order Screen and the other two classes that we created. We need to tie them together.

Solution #1: One easy solution is to create an association between Payment System and Order Screen. In fact, this is actually a valid solution. The Order Screen passes the call to Payment System to process payment. The Payment System returns the result back to Order Screen so that the appropriate message can be displayed. This directional dependency relationship is very typical of classes that use each other's functions. If we do choose this solution, then we inherently make Order Screen the controller of the entire system. A "controller" is a module in the system that orchestrates the behavior of the system; it acts like the brain in the system and tells the other

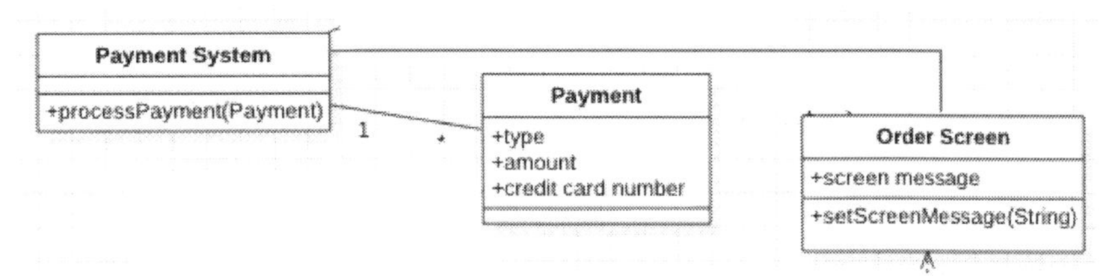

modules in the system what to do.

So, the new overall UML class diagram would be the following:

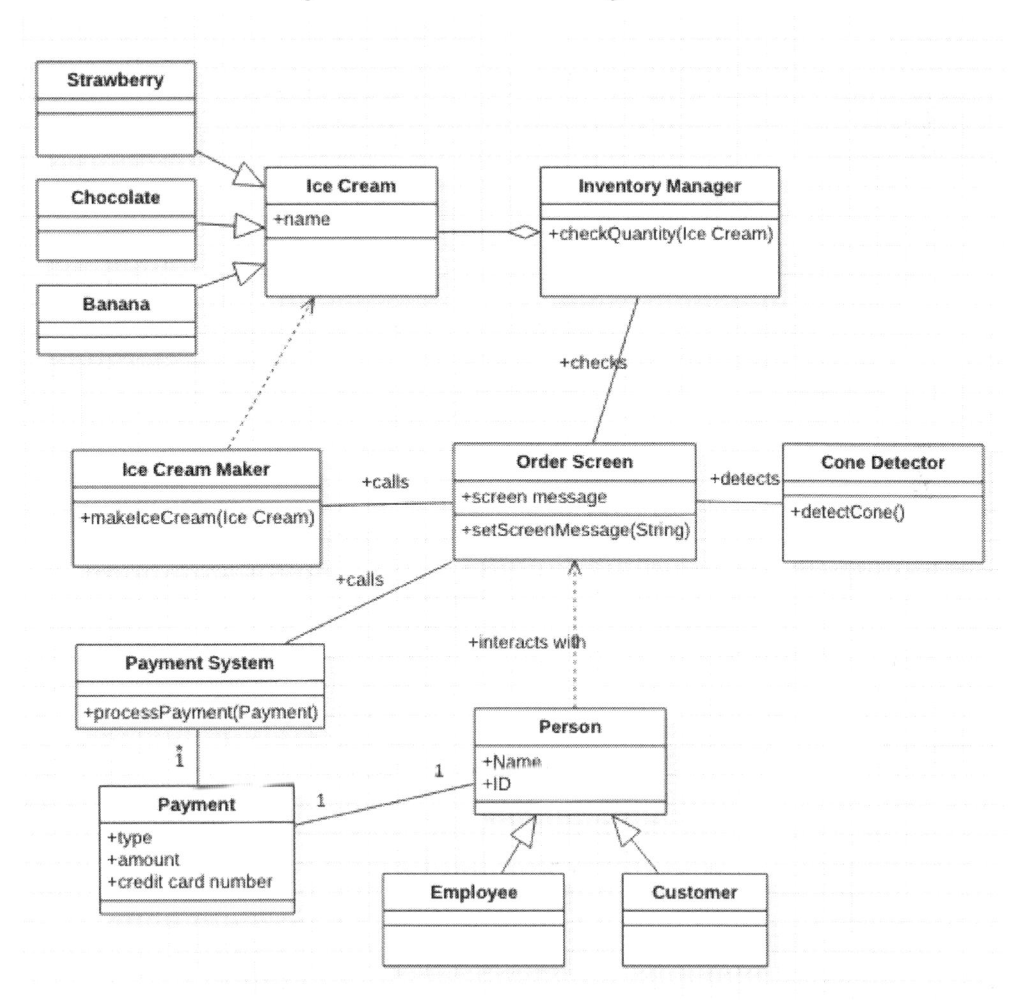

Solution #2: There is another solution that is less obvious. In the UML class diagram that we drew, we had most of the classes interface with Notification System, where the Notification System was basically acting like a conduit or medium to pass messages to each other. This is a more advanced architecture of using a message passing system such as Apache Kafka to have objects put messages into the message queue and other objects listen to those messages and act on them accordingly. This is more of a modern distributed architecture that you would see for a large computer system, not necessarily a small system such as an ice cream machine. But the option is there for you to use it!

Both solutions are correct. One is more extensible than the other but is overkill. One will get the job done more directly. Either solution you choose would be appropriate for the design that satisfies the requirements. Personally though, Solution #1 is the better solution for this type of system.

If we choose Solution #1, how would that change the Architecture Layer Diagram? We would now have 5 modules in the architecture layer diagram, instead of six.

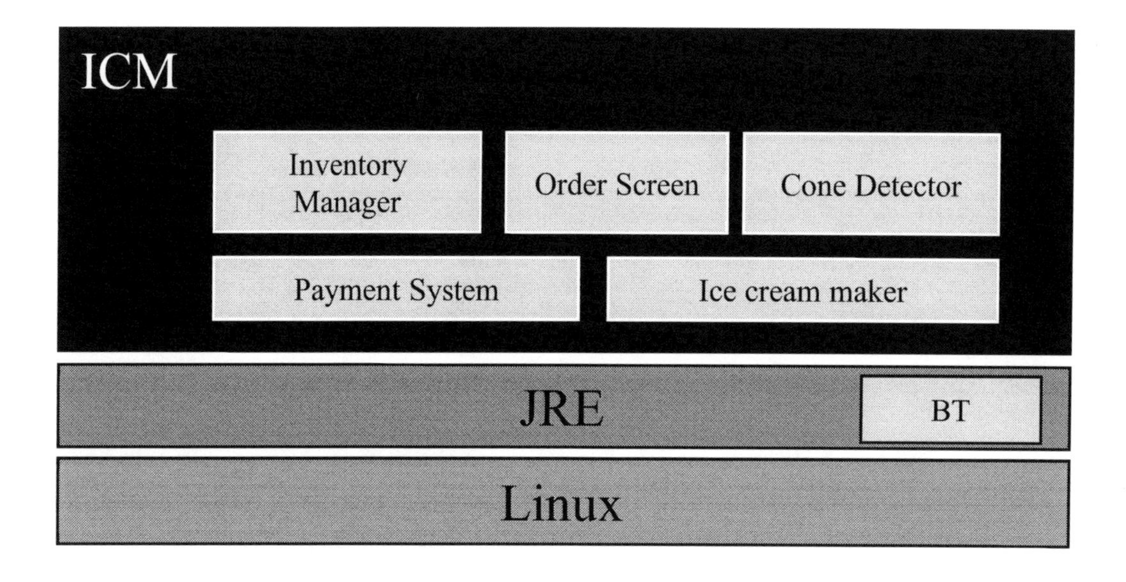

5.1.5 Glossary and Other Items

The final required section of a Design Spec is the glossary. The glossary contains the words and terms and their definitions that we used that we feel that people outside our project would have trouble understanding. Terms or even acronyms like "JRE" are good candidates to be in the Glossary section.

5.2 Exercises

1. What are the five most important elements of a Design Spec?

2. Who is the audience of the Design Spec?

3. What are the top 3 goals of a Design Spec?

4. What else do you think should belong in a Design Specification?

5. Our Design spec of the Ice Cream Machine is missing the Architecture Flow Diagram. Draw the AFD of the Ice Cream Machine.

6. Complete the two remaining features of the Ice Cream Machine. Your UML diagram should look similar to the UML class diagram in the architecture section. In addition to the UML diagram, write the reasoning and logic for why you chose it to design it that way.

7. Imagine that you are tasked to write a Design Spec for a robot toy dog. What are the steps that you would take before you begin writing anything?

[This page left intentionally blank]

6 Use Case to UML

In the previous chapter, we elaborated on the content that goes inside a Design Spec. We actually took an example of an Ice Cream Machine (ICM) selected two of the four features, iterated through a few architecture diagrams, drew several web sequence diagrams, and also iterated through several UML class diagrams until we were happy with our design. The Design Spec is a lot of work and other than code, is one of the most important deliverables of a software engineer.

But there is one thing we skipped over and that is to convert a use case with its requirements to UML. We didn't talk about the process that I used to do this. You had a glimpse of what the process entailed but it wasn't formalized to you.

This chapter formalizes that process of converting use cases and requirements to UML. We call this method the **ABCDFG Method**.

We will work through several exercises to hone in on the skills. If you are simultaneously taking this class, we will also work on a set of different but interesting exercises either individually or as a team and then we get the opportunity to critique each other's designs.

6.1 What is the ABCDFG Method

Recall our ICM use case in the previous chapter. This is the feature that takes in raw materials.

- **Use Case:** ICM machines takes in the raw materials of 3 flavors of ice cream into individualized containers that store the materials. The user is able to check, via the ICM machine screen, how much material is left so that she can add more material when needed. The screen will tell her a specific percentage, one for each of the 3 flavors, ranging from 0% (empty) to 100% (full) in whole number percentages.

How do we convert this to UML?

We use the **ABCDFG Method** in this order.

1. Analyze the User Flow
2. Box the nouns
3. Circle the verbs
4. Document other nouns from (A)
5. Filter the candidates
6. Graph the relationships

The ABCDFG method is a systematic way to convert words into a UML diagram. The first step (A) is to understand the use case and the user flow from end to end. The second step is to draw a box around the nouns found in the use case. Those nouns become candidates for our classes. The third step is to circle the verbs. The verbs are candidates that may become methods in our classes. The fourth step is to look at the nouns and verbs we circled and ask ourselves, are there others that should be candidates but not part of the use case? In step five, we go down the list and filter out the candidates that should not be classes. What we are left with are classes in our UML diagram. Finally, in step 6, we need to determine how the classes are related to each other diagraming the 5 different ways they can be associated with each other.

Let's go into each of the steps in more details.

6.1.1 Analyze the User Flow

In "Analyze the User Flow", we do two main tasks:

1. Understand the user flow from start to end
2. Understand the inputs and outputs

First, we need to understand what the user is doing from start to end. This means that we have to completely understand the use case and possibly even rewrite the use case in chronological order. Chronological is important here because we want to make sure that we don't skip any steps that the user does or doesn't do. We want to make sure we capture every user action whether initiated or not. In the ICM example above, is it written in chronological order? If not, then we need to rewrite it. *(Hint: it is in chronological order).* In fact, the easiest way to test our understanding is to draw a box and pointer diagram of the user flow. We draw the following diagram. Notice that the concept of "Inventory Manager" did not come from the use case, but it came from our understanding of what must happen – the screen needs to get the percentage information from somewhere, so we need an entity that can provide us this information. That entity is the Inventory Manager.

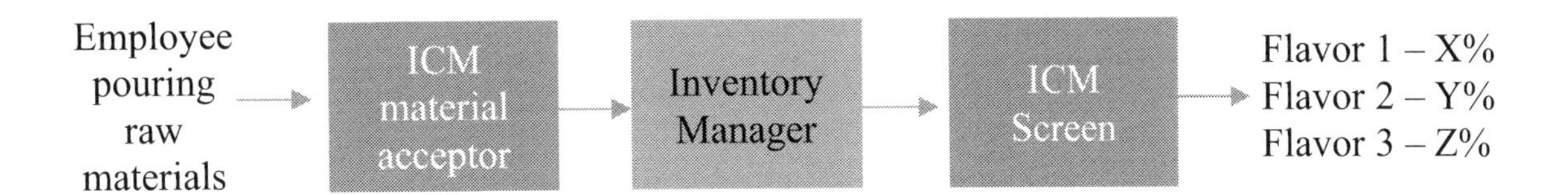

Next, we want to understand the inputs and outputs.

- **Input:** 3 flavors raw materials
- **Output**: 3 output percentages ranging from 0 to 100% for each flavor.
  - *The use case specified output to a screen, but we are going to ignore that for now to simplify.*

The output tells us what our module needs to do, which is to return 3 numbers. Because we are only concerned with the software of the system and not the hardware (i.e. no sensors, containers, raw materials), we assume the hardware is there and can provide us the information that we need. So, we are not concerned about the input in this specific case, just that we need to know that there will be 3 different flavors that ICM supports. Given the information about the input/outputs, it is clear that what we would need to deliver is either 1 or 3 methods to allow the caller to get the 3 pieces of information. But it doesn't give us details about whether this is a class or more classes or not. So, we need to employ the next step.

After Step "A" in ABCDFG Method

Model Candidate List

- Employee
- Ice Cream/Flavor
- Percentage
- Inventory Manager

6.1.2 Box the Nouns

In this second step, we identify all the nouns in the use case and we put a box around it. All the nouns identified becomes a class candidate for our eventual UML class diagram.

Use Case: ICM machines takes in the raw materials of 3 flavors of ice cream into individualized containers that store the materials. The user is able to check, via the ICM machine screen, how much material is left so that she can add more material when needed. The screen will tell her a specific percentage, one for each of the 3 flavors, ranging from 0% (empty) to 100% (full) in whole number percentages.

After Step "B" in ABCDFG Method

Model Candidate List

- ICM Machine
- Ice Cream
- Raw Materials
- Containers
- User
- Screen
- Percentage

6.1.3 Circle the Verbs

In this third step, we identify all the verbs in the use case and we put a circle around it (Alternatively, you can underline it if its more visible to you). All the verbs identified becomes candidates for methods in our eventual UML class diagram.

Use Case: ICM machines takes in the raw materials of 3 flavors of ice cream into individualized containers that store the materials. The user is able to check, via the ICM machine screen, how much material is left so that she can add more material when needed. The screen will tell her a specific percentage, one for each of the 3 flavors, ranging from 0% (empty) to 100% (full) in whole number percentages.

It may be the case that we will have more methods in our UML class diagram than what is listed in the use case. This is typical as the use case may not go into every single interaction in detail. Given what you know so far about methods, which ones do you think are missing?

So far we have

- ICM machines takes in.. / add more material / Containers store materials
- User …check the screen / screen tell percentages

The first three verbs are basically the same as they describe an action to ingest the raw materials. In the system, we model this as an "add" or "set" method. So, we would have method(s) called addMaterials or setMaterials. The second bullet describes an action that allows someone to get the data. In this case, the data is the percentage of material left. So, we would have method(s) such as getRawMaterialsPercentage.

After Step "C" in ABCDFG Method

Model Method List

- addMaterial
- getRawMaterialPercentage

6.1.4 Document other nouns

Step B gave us a list of candidate nouns, but there actually might be more that's not mentioned. We would need to take our analysis in Step A to help us generate any missing nouns. After this step, we would have a complete set of nouns that will compose our candidate class list. So, in Step D, we combine the list in Step A and Step B. This gives us the overall Model Class Candidate List.

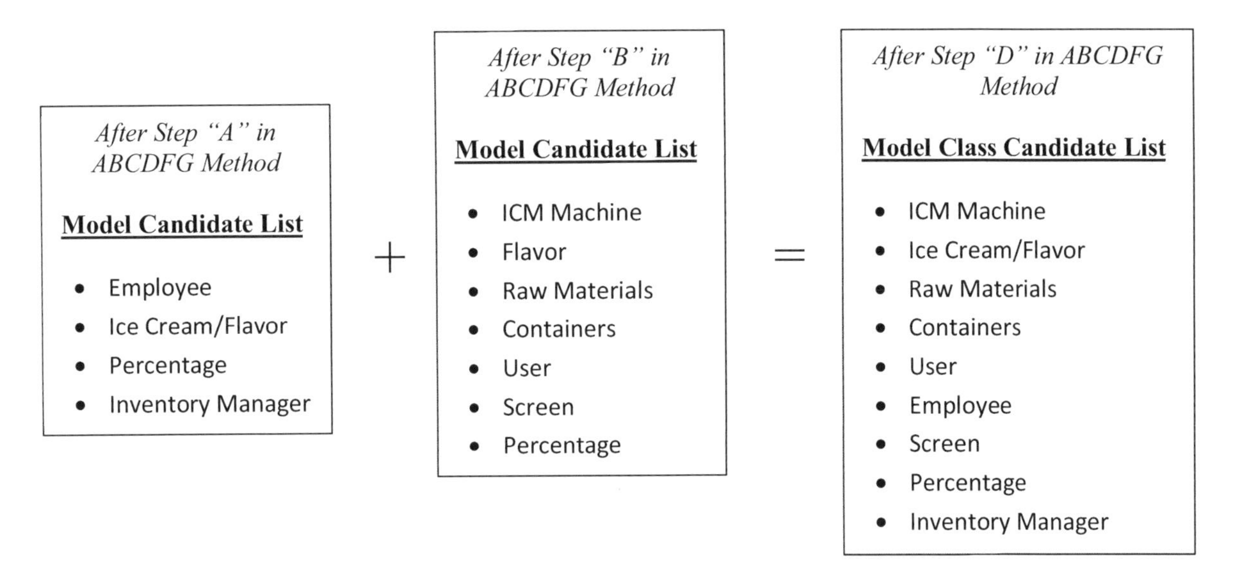

6.1.5 Filter the Candidates

We now have all the candidates and we need to filter the ones that should be represented as classes in our UML class diagram. Let's examine each candidate.

After Step "D" in ABCDFG Method

Model Class Candidate List

- ICM Machine
- Ice Cream/Flavor
- Raw Materials
- Containers
- User
- Employee
- Screen
- Percentage
- Inventory Manager

Could ICM Machine be a class? No, because we are designing the ICM machine, so representing the entire machine as a class wouldn't make sense. We strikeout ICM Machine.

Could Ice Cream/Flavor be a class? We need some way to represent the ice cream flavors so it makes sense that this is a class. Let's label this class "Ice Cream".

Could raw materials be a class? Raw materials would not be a class in our diagram because it basically *is* the ice cream. So, we would have a redundant class. We strikeout Raw Materials.

Could containers be a class? Yes and no. You can make an argument that containers can hold the ice cream and therefore containers should be a class. You can also make an argument that containers could provide the information about the percentage of ice cream left. Those are perfectly valid reasons to make container a class. However, I think there might be a better name or concept to represent as we go down the list. So, let's strike out Containers for now.

Could user (or employee) be a class? Yes! People are almost always represented by one or more classes because it has information that we would use – information like name, id, etc. However, in this particular case, ICM doesn't do anything with the user's information. Nowhere is the user asked to input his or her name. So technically, we can actually leave out User and Employee from the UML diagram and it would be perfectly fine and satisfy the requirements. Technically, all we need is the form of payment, which is tied to the user anyway. But, because users are almost always represented, let's leave it in our UML diagram, but we must fully know that it's perfectly fine to leave it out in this specific example.

Could screen be a class? Yes, because it is operated on by something and has specific tasks that it needs to accomplish.

Could percentage be a class? A percentage is only a number of what's left of the ice cream in the machine. Because it's a number, it's basically a primitive type, so it's best to make this an attribute of a class rather than a class itself.

Finally, could Inventory Manager be a class? Yes, this was the entity that gave us information about the percentage data of the remaining ice cream. We need this concept to help us obtain the information as no class so far is providing it. Technically, the Inventory Manager class and the Container class are basically synonymous because they are the representing class that provides the information about the ice cream percentage.

What are we left with now? 5 classes.

Let's diagram the ice cream flavor first as it's easiest to visualize. Since we have three flavors that we are giving class status to, it makes sense that they share the same superclass. (See previous section on why we decided to make the flavors separate classes).

After Step "F" in ABCDFG Method

Model Class Candidate List

- ~~ICM Machine~~
- Ice Cream/Flavor
- ~~Raw Materials~~
- ~~Containers~~
- User
- Employee
- Screen
- ~~Percentage~~
- Inventory Manager

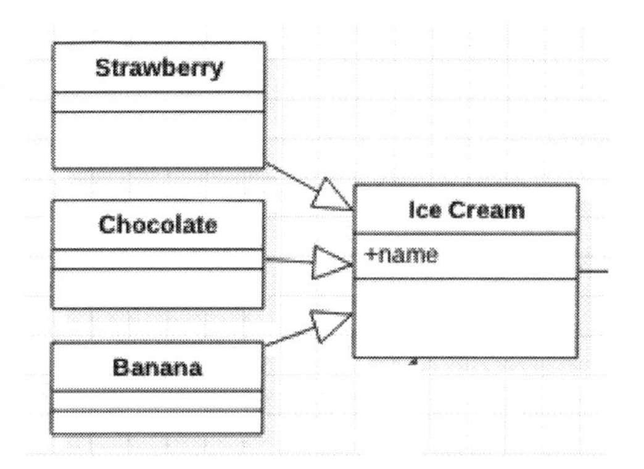

Next, let's diagram the User/Employee. Just like ice cream's inheritance model, we want to do the same with the user and employee with the Person superclass. Realize that nowhere does the name or ID get used by ICM, but we have it here for illustration purposes only.

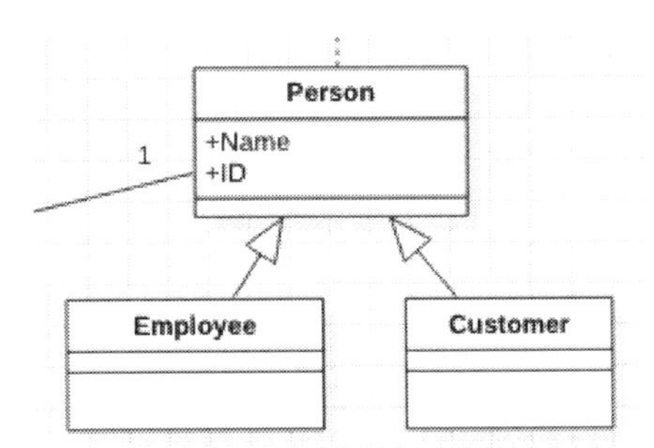

Next, we have the screen. We are actually not given that much information about the screen. Recall Step C's method list, which is copied to the right. None of them apply to Order Screen at all. But I can think of one method that would apply, and that is setScreenMessage because the screen would need some way to get the message to show on the screen!

After Step "C" in ABCDFG Method

Model Method List

- addMaterial
- getRawMaterialPercentage

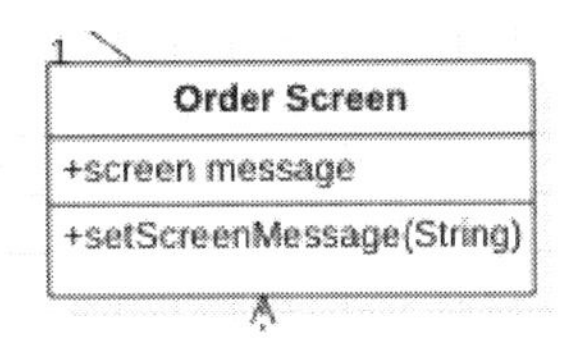

Finally, we have Inventory Manager. It's job is to provide us the remaining ice cream in the form of a percentage. We created a method called checkQuantity that provides the number.

Inventory Manager

+checkQuantity(Ice Cream)

6.1.6 Graph the relationships

The last step requires us to determine the relationships or associations between each of the classes that we identified. The diagram below represents our understanding of how each of the classes are associated. As we note again, the Person class "interacting" or dependency relationship with Order Screen is really a "on the surface" association. Technically, we don't need to draw this relationship because there is no technical relationship between the two. However, as we are starting out diagraming, it's best to show at least how Person would interact with Order Screen if the Person were required to input his name into the screen.

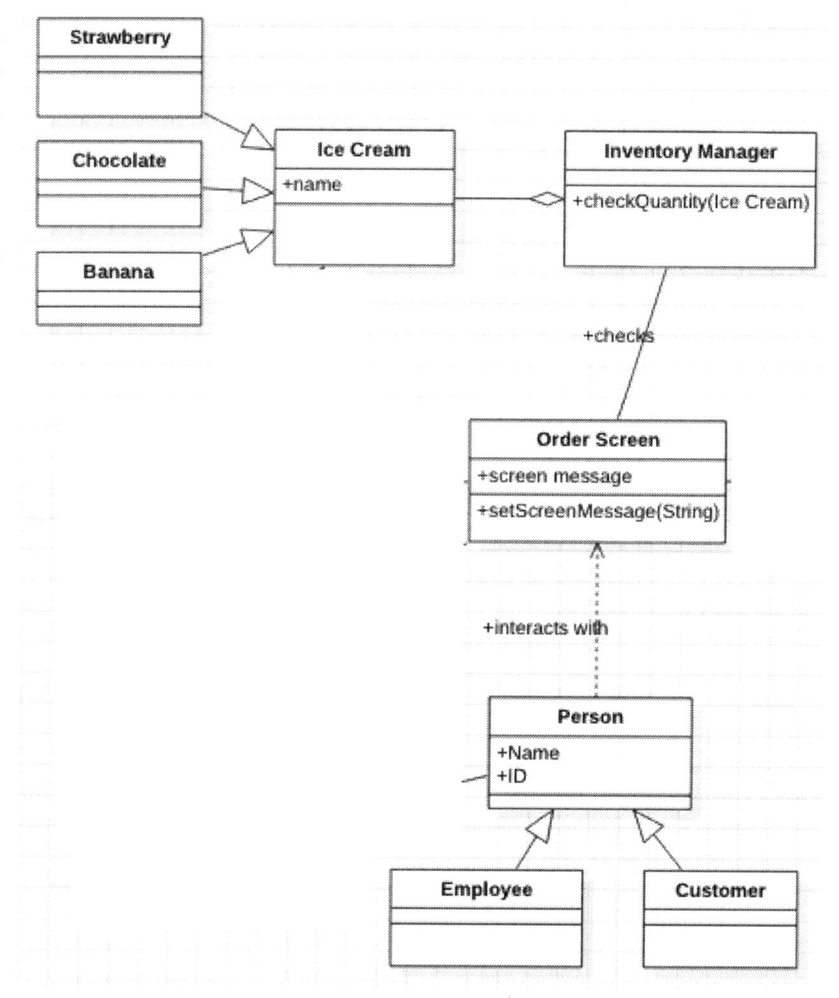

6.2 Applying ABCDFG – Example #2

Let's do one more example with the ICM machine to make sure we understand the principles of the ABCDFG Method. We are going to use a familiar use case that we completed a UML diagram before, but this time we will make sure we apply the ABCDFG method.

> *Use Case: Customer looks at ICM and sees the screen say "Select a Flavor then press Order". Customer selects a flavor, sees it confirmed on the screen, and then presses the order button to confirm the order. He is then prompted to pay with a credit card. After he inserts the credit card, it processes the payment and he takes his card back. Screen will then display "Making Ice Cream!"*

Analyze the User Flow

Instead of a box pointer diagram, we are going to use a sequence diagram to document the flows because the use case is actually pretty interactive and goes back and forth between ICM and the user.

Here's what the sequence diagram looks like. We've included four different actors in our diagram: Screen, User, Button and Payment System. We added Button, which is a specific actor, instead of a concept like

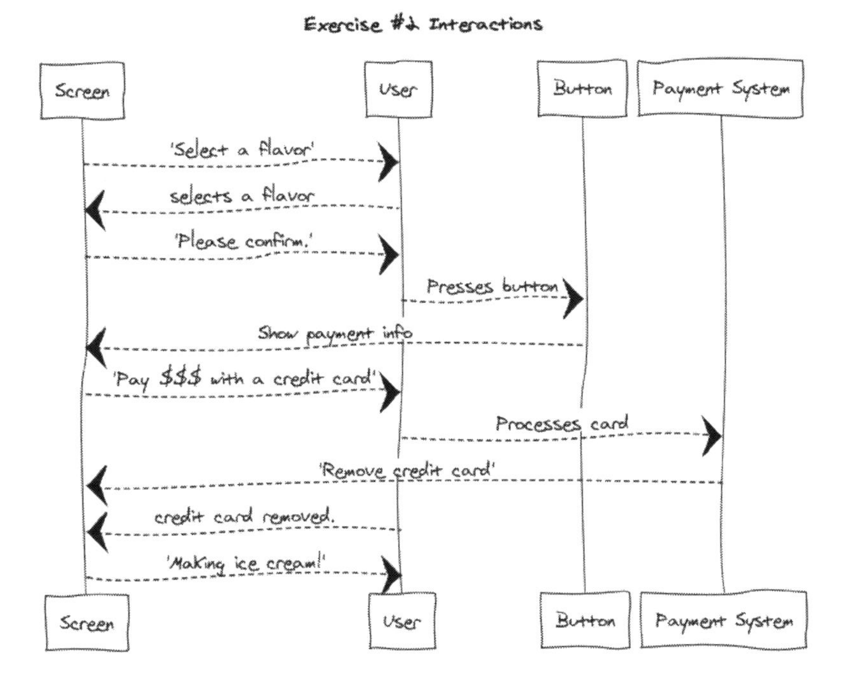

"ICM Machine" because we want to be a little bit more specific – after all we are building the ICM Machine! We also included Payment System as an actor and used it for both hardware and software purposes. That's OK to do, as long as you fully understand that there is also a hardware component to it, which we don't model anyways.

So, what does the sequence diagram tell us? It told us a series of inputs and outputs and also the processes that happen in between. Let's document them:

- **Input:**
    - Flavor selection by user
    - Button confirmation
    - Payment with credit card
    - Removal of credit card
- **Output**:
    - Text on the screen showing the result of the inputs
        - "Select a Flavor"
        - "Please Confirm"
        - "Pay with $$$ Credit Card"
        - "Remove Credit Card"
        - "Making Ice Cream"
- **Process** (which may translate to methods)
    - Process user flavor selection
    - Process user confirmation selection
    - Process user payment
    - Process user removal of card

Given the above, we have a list of model class candidates:

After Step "A" in ABCDFG Method

Model Candidate List

- Customer
- Ice Cream/Flavor
- Payment/Credit Card
- Button

So, what does the sequence diagram tells us that doing a box and pointer won't? You can actually do it any way you would like and in fact, it would be beneficial to do both. Both will tell you the inputs and outputs, but the sequence diagram will tell you more about what goes on inside the black box.

Box the nouns

Given the use case, we identify all the nouns.

> **Use Case:** Customer looks at ICM and sees the screen say "Select a Flavor then press Order". Customer selects a flavor, sees it confirmed on the screen, and then presses the order button to confirm the order. He is then prompted to pay with a credit card. After he inserts the credit card, it processes the payment and he takes his card back. Screen will then display "Making Ice Cream!"

After Step "B" in ABCDFG Method

Model Candidate List

- Customer
- Ice Cream
- Screen
- Payment/Credit Card

Circle the verbs

Given the use case, we identify the verbs just like in the previous example.

> **Use Case:** Customer looks at ICM and sees the screen say "Select a Flavor then press Order". Customer selects a flavor, sees it confirmed on the screen, and then presses the order button to confirm the order. He is then prompted to pay with a credit card. After he inserts the credit card, it processes the payment and he takes his card back. Screen will then display "Making Ice Cream!"

After Step "C" in ABCDFG Method

Model Method List

- selectFlavor(Ice Cream)
- confirmOrder(Ice Cream)
- pay(Payment)

Notice that we didn't list "customer looks at ICM" and "he inserts the credit card.." verbs as part of the method list because the customer takes those actions that the system does not directly see. In fact, the "insert" method is essentially the pay() method.

Document other nouns from (A)

We combine our work in Step A and B to get the final class candidate list.

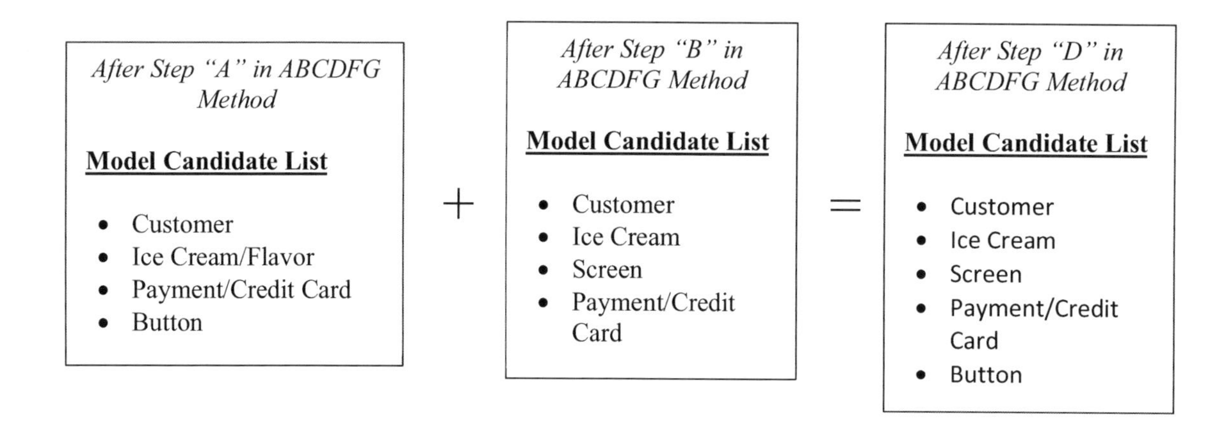

Filter the candidates

Next, we take the result of Step D and filter out the concepts that won't make it into our UML class diagram.

After Step "F" in ABCDFG Method

Model Candidate List

- Customer
- Ice Cream
- Screen
- Payment/Credit Card
- ~~Button~~

The only candidate class that didn't make it to the list is Button. User Interface (UI) components usually don't make it to the UML class diagram unless the context of the UML class diagram is strictly about the UI.

Graph the relationships

So, we have the 4 classes and we have the UML diagram from Exercise #1. Let's combine them into one monolithic UML class diagram. And we are done!

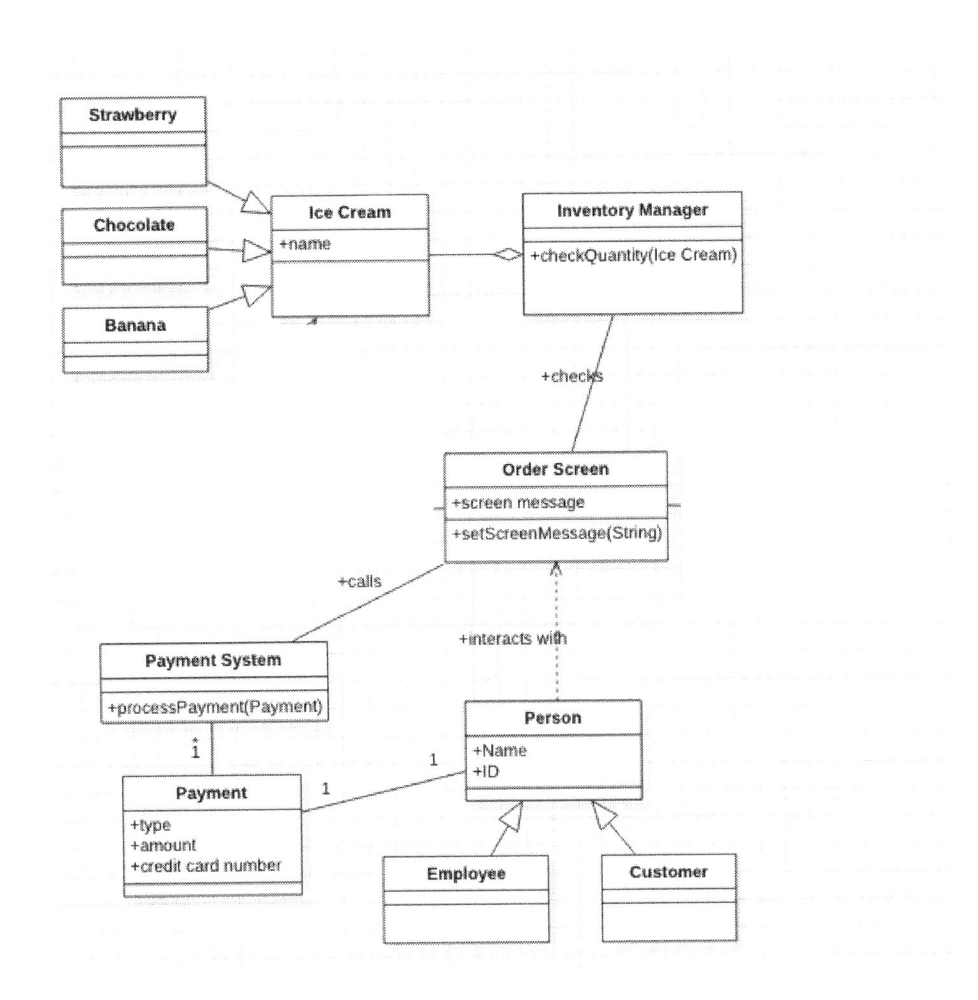

6.3 Applying ABCDFG – Example #3

Let's do one more example, but this time use a topic that is completely different.

Problem: You are a software engineer for a leading electronic payments company. You allow merchants and online stores to embed your software on their mobile devices such that their customers can shop and pay on their mobile phones. You are in charge of the service that processes the payment details when the merchant's app sends you the information. Customers can pay using their credit card, PayPal account, bank account, or debit card.

Suppose there is a Mobile app called WallyMart that has embedded your company's code that packages the call to your company's payment processor in the cloud. We call the package an SDK. The SDK is responsible for packaging the call and return results. The call consists of the form of payment (one of the four as identified above), the payment amount, the details of the payment such as credit card number or account number, expiration date if required, and security code if required. The payment processor in the cloud returns the result whether the payment was successful or not.

Design the payment processor system (PPS) in the cloud. Draw the UML class diagram. (Tip: Only concern yourself with the functionality. Do not include the SDK.)

> **Use Case:** User is shopping on the WallyMart mobile app. She is ready to checkout. Her total amount is $44.12. She decides to use a credit card. She enters the details in the required form. After she is done entering, she presses "Place Order" to finalize and place the order. PPS is called by the WallyMart app with the appropriate information. PPS processes the payment details and returns a success code so that WallyMart can interpret that as a successful transaction. WallyMart presents to the user a "Thank You – your order has been successfully placed" message.

Solution: This example does not require you to understand how payment systems work in detail because the use case provided includes all the context and necessary info for you. What do we do when given a problem like this? We use the ABCDFG Method.

Analyze the User Flow

Make sure you understand the question (Draw the UML class diagram of the PPS system only) and the use case. For this specific example, a sequence diagram appears to be the most appropriate for us to deeply understand because there are just so many calls and returns back and forth. A box and pointer diagram will only give us the ins-and-outs, which may not give us the complete picture.

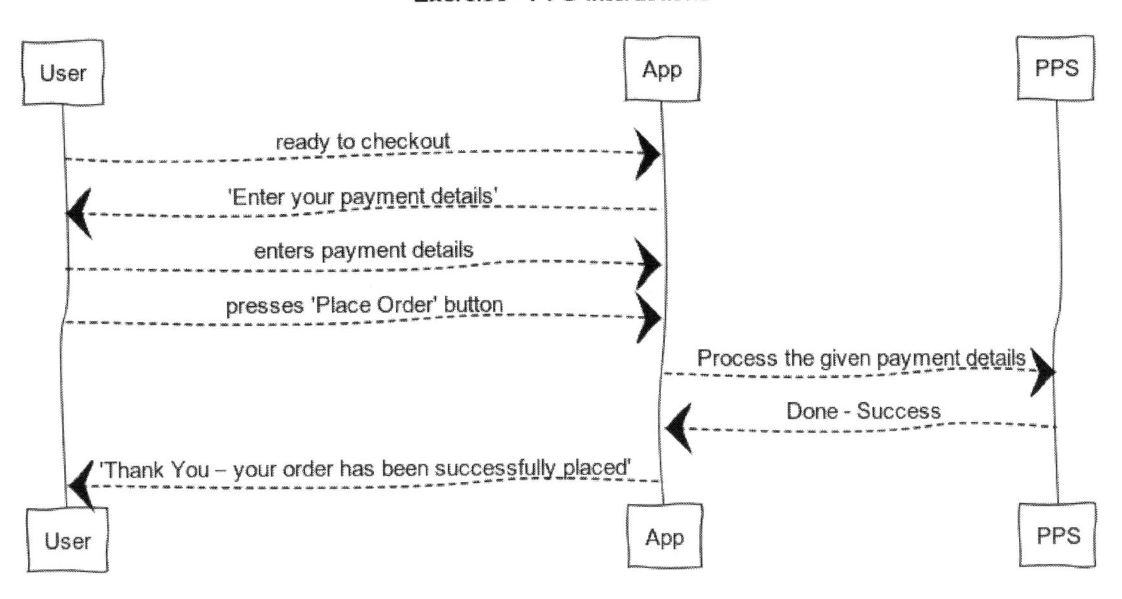

There are 3 actors – User, App, and PPS. The first two can be candidates, but the last one (PPS) is the system we are designing. We know from the use case that PPS accepts Payment and does some processing, so let's make both concepts candidate classes. We arrive at the following list below.

After Step "A" in ABCDFG Method

Model Candidate List

- User
- App
- Payment
- Payment Processor

Box the nouns

Given the use case, we identify all the nouns.

> **Use Case:** User is shopping on the WallyMart mobile app. She is ready to checkout. Her total amount is $44.12. She decides to use a credit card. She enters the details in the required form. After she is done entering, she presses "Place Order" to finalize and place the order. PPS is called by the WallyMart app with the appropriate information. PPS processes the payment details and returns a success code so that WallyMart can interpret that as a successful transaction. WallyMart presents to the user a "Thank You – your order has been successfully placed" message.

After Step "B" in ABCDFG Method

Model Candidate List

- User
- App
- amount
- Payment details/type - Credit Card, Debit card, bank account, PayPal
- PPS

Circle the verbs

Given the use case, we identify the verbs just like in the previous example. You will notice that the sequence diagram that we did above gives us very similar results.

> **Use Case:** User is shopping on the WallyMart mobile app. She is ready to checkout. Her total amount is $44.12. She decides to use a credit card. She enters the details in the required form. After she is done entering, she presses "Place Order" to finalize and place the order. PPS is called by the WallyMart app with the appropriate information. PPS processes the payment details and returns a success code so that WallyMart can interpret that as a successful transaction. WallyMart presents to the user a "Thank You – your order has been successfully placed" message.

After Step "C" in ABCDFG Method

Model Method List

- Checkout
- Decides to use payment
- Enters details
- Presses Place Order
- PPS is called
- PPS processes
- App presents to the user a message

Document other nouns from (A)

We combine our work in Step A and B to get the final class candidate list.

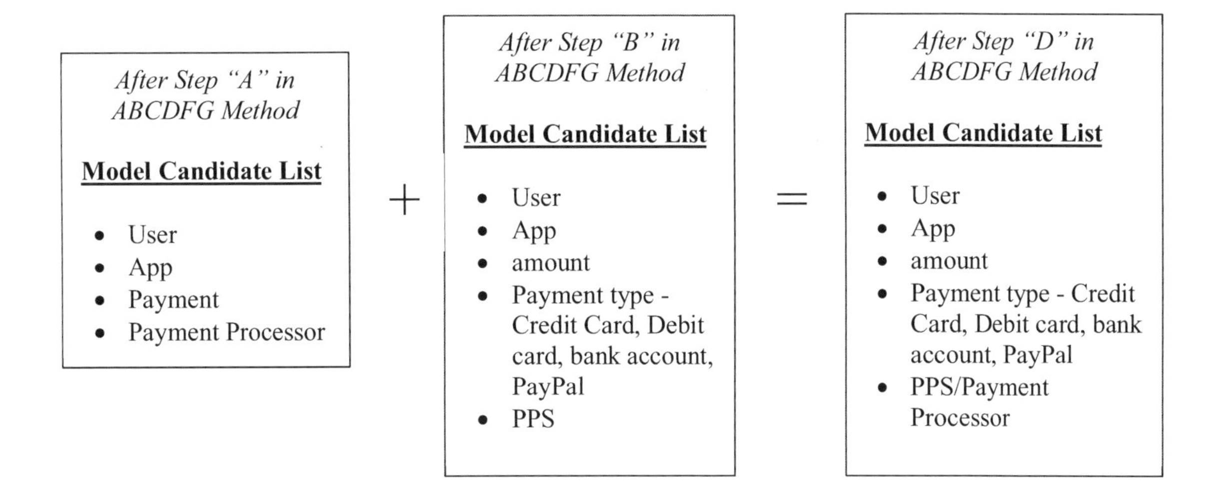

Filter the candidates

Next, we take the result of Step D and filter out the concepts that won't make it into our UML class diagram.

After Step "D" in ABCDFG Method

Model Candidate List

- ~~User~~
- App
- ~~amount~~
- Payment type - Credit Card, Debit card, bank account, PayPal
- PPS/Payment Processor

The candidate classes that didn't make it to the list are "User" and "amount". Amount is a number – a primitive – and part of the Payment details. For user, we are not given much info about the User. In fact, the user details such as the name on the credit card or account are most likely embedded in the payment details. Nowhere does it say that the payment processor will store any user information.

We included App – the WallyMart Mobile App – for placeholder purposes. We don't include any details about the App and it technically is not a class in our UML class diagram.

Graph the relationships

Before we draw the UML diagram, we need to filter out the methods in Step C. Some of the methods are App actions, so we need to strike them out. We only want to keep the methods that is related directly to the system we are building.

PPS is called and PPS processes are the same, and the return result of that call is the "app presenting" the message back to the user.

After Step "C" in ABCDFG Method

Model Method List

- ~~Checkout~~
- ~~Decides to use payment~~
- ~~Enters details~~
- ~~Presses Place Order~~
- PPS is called
- PPS processes
- App presents to the user a message

So, we have the following UML class diagram.

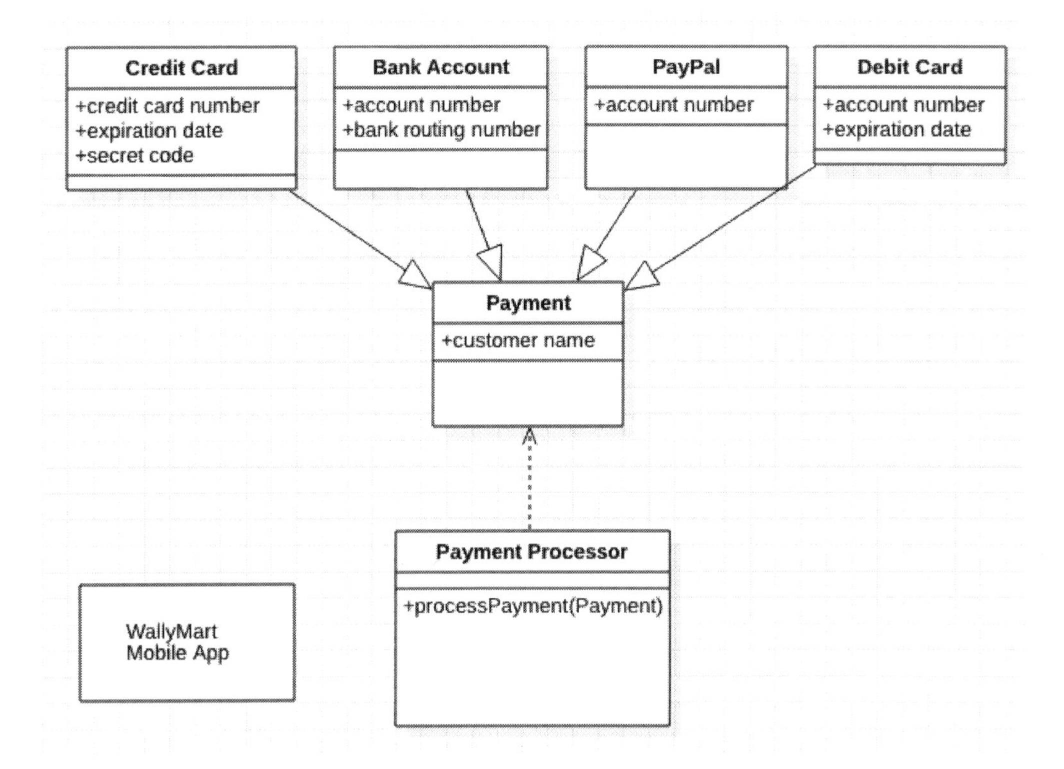

[This page left intentionally blank]

6.4 Exercises

1. What is the ABCDFG Method?

2. In the last example, Example #3, modify the UML diagram to accommodate the following:
    a. Imagine that the payment processing company wants to expand their service from payments to providing loans. This new service, called Loan Processing Service, does the following: takes the user name and his/her credit score and outputs the maximum loan in dollars that she can borrow.

    b. Expanding (a) above, make this new service take in the annual income as another input.

    c. Instead of the user name, annual income, and credit score, they decided to change all of this and instead use a "User's Profile" instead, which contains all this information about the user. Change the UML diagram to accommodate User Profile instead.

3. Imagine that you are the lead architect for a bicycling company called Pelotony. They make exercise bikes with large monitors that connect with exercise instructors and other cyclists around the world. Your job is to design a UML diagram for the following use cases:

    Use Case #1: A user logs into Pelotony using the screen while sitting on the bike. He types his user name and password. When he logs in, he sees a dashboard of his past rides. Each past ride shows the duration (how long he cycled), distance (how far), and average speed. He also sees an aggregate of all the rides he's done this year; the aggregate information is total distance and total time he spent on the bike.

    Use Case #2: A user is able to pick an instructor before each ride if he so chooses. Once he picks an instructor, that instructor leads him through the exercise for the entire duration. An instructor could also be a rider on Pelotony.

4. Forget Pelotony. We are going to make something much better. We will call this the UltimateExerciser, which is a treadmill, exercise bike, and lifting weight machine all in one. A user can do one of the 3 types of exercises. Each exercise has its own programs. A program is marked by level of difficulty. So, a Level 1 program will be easier than a Level 10 program. A user will need to pick one of the programs before she starts exercising. A user's exercise records are stored and she can look them up later in the account history. Draw a UML diagram for this part of the software.

5. Imagine that you are the lead architect for Google Search. This is your product:

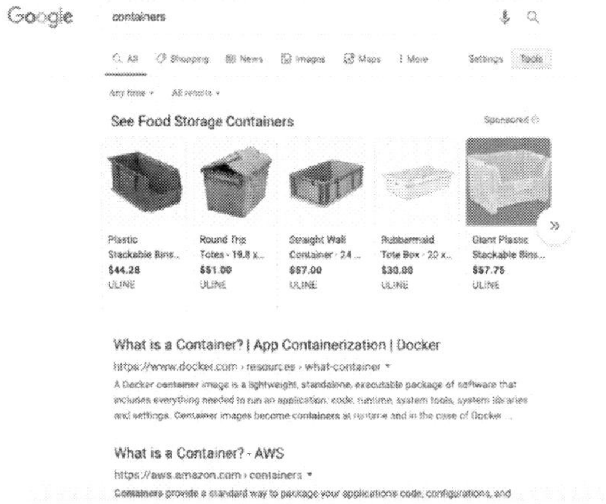

You are tasked with designing a new feature that categorizes the results. So, when you search for "Containers", instead of getting the following results:

You get the results to the right instead. Essentially, you have a new way to filter the results based on the attributes of the returned results. So, if the container results have attribute types of color and size, then the user would be able to filter on it.

Design a UML class diagram that satisfies the requirement. *(Hint: Apply the ABCDFG Method. In the absence of a given user case, create one using the data provided.)*

Images/screenshots from Google.com.

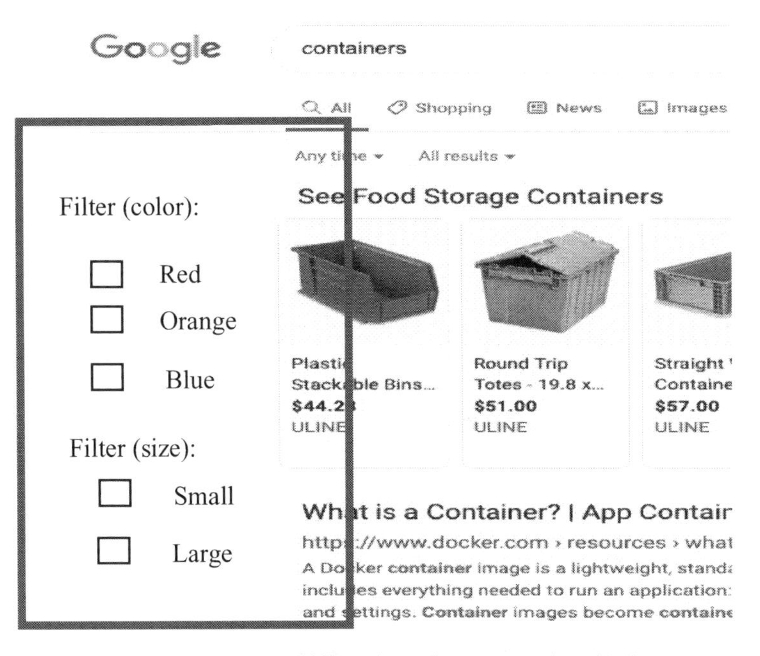

7 Precursor to Design Principles

Before we step into the land of Design Principles, there's a few more foundational topics that we need to learn.

- Object Oriented Programming Language Standard Features
    - Objects vs Classes
    - Inheritance
    - Encapsulation
    - Polymorphism
    - Information Hiding
- Real World Modeling
- Responsibility vs Data Driven Design
- Criticisms of Object-Oriented Paradigm

The first set of topics below are not design principles, but they are inherent features to object oriented programming languages. All true object-oriented programming languages will exhibit those behaviors in one form or another.

The second set of topics deal with real world modeling, where you could imagine a world absent of design principles, how would you go about designing your software. This is an important topic that you should know as it offers another complementary paradigm to object oriented design.

The third topic is a controversial (yes, controversy does exist in computer science as it relates to how people should approach solving problems) area in design. Should you model your design based on its responsibilities (that the design principles espouse) or should you model your design based on how the data is encapsulated?

Finally, the fourth topic is another controversial area. Not everyone is on board with the object-oriented paradigm and you should know why so that you learn the pitfalls and arguments for and against the object-oriented paradigm.

7.1 OO Programming Language Standard Features

Remember, the object-oriented paradigm is all about creating objects. Our job is to determine the best way to create them that is logical, reasonable, and that leads to code maintainability, extensibility, and other benefits. That's it. And along that way to determining the "best way to create them" we meet people and places (i.e. concepts) that help us refine what that means. Concepts like inheritance, encapsulation, responsibilities, etc., teach us how to be better designers. More advanced topics like design principles and design patterns help us be even better designers. But let's focus on the basics for a moment to make sure we have a solid grounding; this is what this section is about.

7.1.1 What is the difference between Objects and Classes?

Understanding the difference between objects and classes is an important distinction. A class is a blueprint or a skeleton. An object is an instantiation of the class.

If you are an architect and you in charge of architecting a house, one of your deliverables is the blueprint of the house. The blueprint tells other people working on the project what the house looks like and what it does. But you can't walk into that blueprint and you can't physically touch the house because it only exists on paper.

The blueprint diagram on the right shows the layout of the house. But it's not tangible because it only exists on paper.

The instantiation of the class, or the creation of the house, is taking that blueprint and actually building the house. When a class is instantiated, it exists in the computer's memory (RAM) so that it becomes interactable.

7.1.2 Inheritance

All object-oriented programming languages come with a feature called inheritance. Inheritance establishes a parent-child relationship between two classes where the child class **"inherits" or takes attributes and methods from the parent class**. The child class becomes a subtype class.

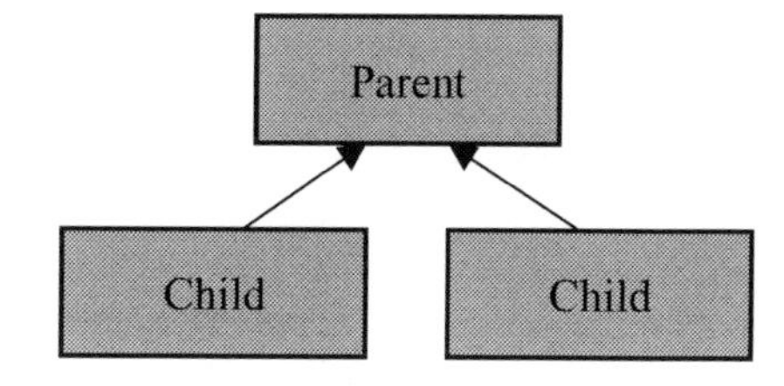

This parent has two children.

But the child does not necessarily need to inherit everything about its parent. The child can overwrite attributes and methods; the child could say "Mom/Dad, I actually don't like the way you cook, so I'm going cook a different way." By overwriting, the child establishes a new way of doing (method) or being (attribute) something.

Through inheritance, you can also specify a pretty deep inheritance tree and make this as many levels as you desire.

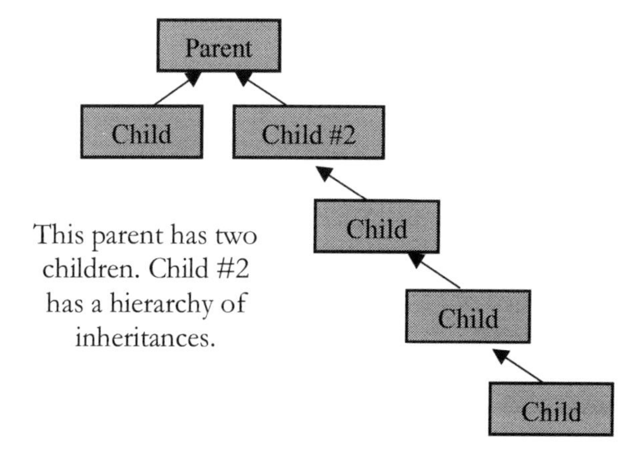

This parent has two children. Child #2 has a hierarchy of inheritances.

The following three pieces of code specifies a parent and child relationship two levels deep. The parent is class Car. Car has a set of 3 attributes and 3 methods. Let's say that we create a new class Toyota that inherits from Car. This makes sense because Toyota is a brand of cars and so Toyota doesn't want to re-create the wheel (literally and figuratively). So, Toyota is going to customize Car its own way. It's going to add a new attribute, length, and specify how the car is started, and a new method to reverse. Toyota has a car model called Camry. Camry is a sedan so it would need attributes and methods that are specific to it. It wouldn't make sense for Camry to inherit directly from Car, because if it did that, it would bypass any special configurations that Toyota had established. You only want to inherit from the parent if it makes sense to do so, where it minimizes code redundancy and follows a logical order (i.e. Camry is a type of Toyota so Toyota should be Camry's direct parent).

```
class Car {
   attributes: color, doors, speed
   methods: start, forward, stop
}
```

```
class Toyota extends Car {
   attributes:
      color,
      doors,
      speed,
      length
   methods:
      start = physical key
required,
      forward,
      stop,
      reverse
}
```

```
class Camry extends Toyota {
   attributes:
      color,
      doors,
      speed,
      length,
      seat_comfort_level,
      center_of_gravity
   methods:
      start,
      forward,
      stop,
      reverse,
      playRadio,
      playAppleCarRadio
}
```

7.1.3 Encapsulation

Although not unique to object-oriented paradigm, encapsulation represents two processes:

- Putting together data and method as one concept, and
- Hiding information and only exposing methods to get access to it

In the former, the result of applying the "encapsulation" process is a class. You want to bundle the appropriate attributes/data with the right methods into one entity. So, given a Social Security Number, Credit Card Number, Name, and Address with methods of talking, walking, sleeping, and eating, you may decide to coagulate those attributes and methods together into a concept called Person because all those things are what a real-life person is and does.

Another way to think about it is this. Imagine you are a chemist charged with creating this one pill with a single purpose to extend life expectancy by 20 years. Your job is to come up with attributes and methods of this and you have to encapsulate it all into one tiny pill. Your job is difficult because you have to find the right attributes/methods that serves its purpose.

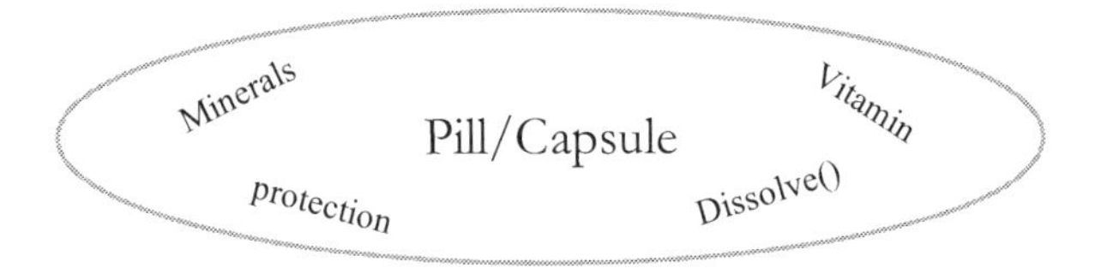

For information hiding, the idea is to only expose attributes and methods as required. You do this in several ways:

- Use of language specific keywords
- Use of getter and setter methods

The first way is to make use of special keywords supplied by the programming language of choice. In Java, you can use "private", "public", "protected" to specify the visibility of the attribute or method.

The second way is that once you've made something private, you'll want a way to have others externally access it, if that's something that you want to do. Getters and/or setter methods satisfy this requirement by only creating those types of methods for the attributes or methods you want to restrict access to.

In the below example, we made all the attributes "private" and exposed the attributes via methods. Notice how you cannot set the SSN externally because no public method exists.

```
class Person {
   private SSN;
   private name;
   private address;

   public getSSN() { .. }
   public getName() { .. }
   public setName(name) { .. }
   public changeAddress(address) { .. }
}
```

7.1.4 Polymorphism

Polymorphism is the use of a single entity to represent multiple different types. The prefix "Poly" means many and the word "morph" means shape. So, polymorphism means many shapes.

There are three main forms of polymorphism.

- **Ad-hoc polymorphism** – where multiple methods of the same name are defined but the difference is in the parameters of the methods. Polymorphism allows this and the programming language decides which method to call based on the types.

```
class Confusing {
        int add(Integer a, Integer b) {
                print "add Integers";
        }
        int add(String c, String d) {
                print "add Strings";
        }
}
```

  So, if you did this:

```
Confusing c = new Confusing();
c.add(new Integer(1), new Integer(2));
c.add("3", "4");
```

  The output would be:

```
add Integers
add Strings
```

- **Parametric polymorphism** – where the type doesn't matter so the method can handle any types. In JAVA, it is the use of generics as follows:

```
List<Book> books = new ArrayList<Book>();
```

  This way when you call any method in Book class, the precise method is called based on which type (or sub-type) of Book it is. This saves you from type-casting if you didn't use generics.

  Method overloading, the process of creating another method with the same name but different parameters, is an example of parametric polymorphism.

- **Subtype polymorphism** – where the method accepts the subtype of the type. This is achieved through inheritance. So, if you execute the code in the examples below, depending on the type, it will print out the appropriate message when called.

  Method overriding, the process of creating the same method in the sub-class (same name and same parameters) and overwriting the implementation of the super class, is an example of subtype polymorphism.

```
interface Book {
   void checkout();
}

class Magazine extends Book {
   void checkout() { print "Magazine!"; }
}

class AudioBook extends Book {
   void checkout() { print "Ears only!"; }
}
```

```
Book foo = new Magazine();
Book bar = new
AudioBook();

foo.checkout(); // prints
"Magazine!"

bar.checkout(); // prints
"Ears only!"
```

7.1.5 Information Hiding

Information hiding is about showing the right amount of details externally and hiding all the other details. Here are some examples:

- I'm a large online retailer and I hold all the product information which I want to sell in a database. I also hold information about my customer's payment information like credit cards and address.
    - I (the online retailer) should only expose product information that a customer would find useful such as the product name, price, description, and quantity; I do not want to expose how much I paid for the product that I'm selling you. That is information hiding.
    - I (the online retailer) will block out all requests for any customer's payment information unless that request came directly from the customer accessing his own data. Blocking out the request is information hiding.
- I'm a bank. I will only expose to customers what they could only do at a bank such as withdraw or deposit money or obtain a loan. If a customer inquires about what happens to the money when they deposit it, I will respond that the money is in the bank, but the truth is that that money is being used to lend out to other people. That truth is information hiding. All the customer needs to know is that if she needs the money, it will be there; she doesn't need to know that the bank used 10% of her deposit to fund a loan for someone else to buy a house.

There is a big difference between information hiding and encapsulation. We saw the definition of encapsulation and although the process of implementing each may be the same via specialized keywords, the thought process is slightly different.

Information hiding deals with the interface level and not just creating getters and setter methods. It's about creating a well-defined interface of what a client can do or not do. Whereas encapsulation is more about wrapping up the data and methods into a package so that it can be represented in a class and behave in a way consistent with the actions of the class.

Information hiding goes a step further with an interface class that defines these actions that can occur.

```
interface Bank {
   deposit(money)
   withdraw(money)
   getLoan(amount)
   closeAccount()
}

class BankOfAmerica extends Bank {

   // defines the methods of the interface here


}
```

7.2 Real World Modeling

One of the most important ideas about Object Oriented Paradigm is that if we model our design after the real world, then our design automatically is efficient, because the real world – specifically nature – is highly efficient. When you start decomposing the elements of nature and wrap each concept in a class, it becomes almost apparent, sometimes obvious, that that is the way that you should have designed your software.

Let's design a simple dining table using the real-world method.

What does this table have? A typical flat table top and four legs. What does your UML class diagram look like? Take a few minutes to come up with a design.

Did you draw something like this?

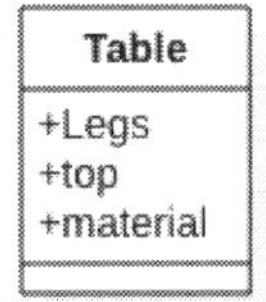

Or did you draw something like this?

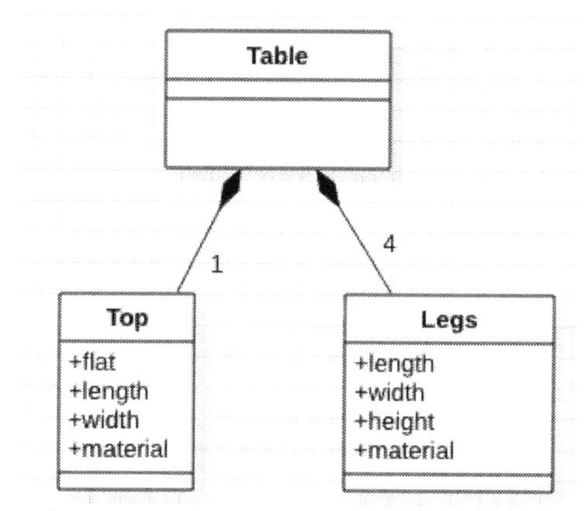

The result of using the real-world method would have been the latter because the table is composed of those elements. Someone has to cut the top and someone has to cut and make the 4 legs. That's exactly how the table is constructed in real life.

The method is simple: copy what occurs in the real world.

This idea of modeling your software after the real world is not new and also faces criticism. Some critics say that not everything can be modelled after the real world, and that not everything is efficient. They are correct, but that's if a literal viewpoint of the idea is taken. You will obviously want to tweak the design so that it fits your requirements and you will want to fashion it in ways that make it amenable to modularity, maintainability, and extensibility. Using the real-world method, you'll have to think hard about what a table (or any concept for that matter) exposes in terms of methods, information hiding, and other concepts that we've learned.

7.3 Criticisms of OOP

OOP is not perfect; no software engineering paradigm is. OOP is like a way of life, it's a methodology, it's a way of doing something to achieve a goal. And as with anything that espouses a particular way of doing something, it will be subject to scrutiny, criticism, and isolationism.

As you continue your studies of OOP, you should know what others say or think about it. Not that you have to defend OOP, but that you should think that perhaps, their comments might actually be valid, and because it might be valid, it might change the way that you design your code to make it even better.

… you should think that perhaps, their comments might actually be valid, and because it might be valid, it might change the way that you design your code to make it even better …

Here are some criticisms that have been bestowed on OOP:

- Doesn't actually lead to more modular code
- Doesn't actually make code easier to program
- Doesn't actually increase reuse

There are a lot more criticisms and some have equated OOP to (gasp) snake oil. I find it rather disconcerting that a particular way of doing something has garnered so strong an opinion on some people. I think the main issue has been the over promise of OOP and perhaps the lack of understanding of how to best use the principles. As an example, if you borrow any OOP book from the library or your favorite book store, the definitions and examples, as you will discover, are vague or don't explain the material well. The lack of examples and the use of the same words to explain the definition of the word being defined (i.e. "abstraction is when a particular module is abstracted to solve a problem") means nothing to students. This is one of the reasons why I decided to write this book and save my own students from the perils of a lacking book.

Now, let's take one of the criticisms above and see how valid or not valid it is:

> *"OOP doesn't actually make code easier to program"*

Why the statement is valid: The statement that OOP makes code more difficult to program can be true because the programmer must first understand OOP. If the programmer does not understand OOP, then it becomes a near lost cause to write, change, or delete code. Now, if the programmer is well versed in OOP and still finds it difficult to navigate the code base, it could be for the following reasons: large code base, code base that is assumed to OOP but is not, design principles that were broken or not followed.

First, a large code base, regardless of the software engineering paradigm used, will be difficult to navigate no matter what. Even people who have written the code all by themselves find it difficult to go back several years later to find where they should modify the code to add a new feature. This is not an OOP specific problem.

Second, a code base that "looks like OOP" but is not is another problem. Regardless of how the codebase got into that state, the fact that it is not true OOP may make things more difficult for the programmer. Imagine if you used a mix of functional and OOP paradigms in the code, it could sometimes be confusing (and this does exist).

Third, when design principles are not followed, ignored, or broken, it may make the code even more confusing and convoluted. This is why design principles exist to formalize the design.

As you can see, the statement could be true and the naysayers have it sometimes right.

Why the statement is false: If OOP code is written well, guidelines are followed, design principles are followed to the dot, falling into an abyss of OOP code becomes less likely but not impossible. There could be many reasons and one reason that I cited above is that large code bases (think millions of lines of code and more) make things much more complex. In fact, code bases are becoming more and more complex due to the sheer number of people and coding styles working on the code. Large corporations with multi-national, cross time zones development teams work on the code 24 hours a day, code is constantly changing, so who makes sure that the code adheres to one set of stringent guidelines and enforces it in the face of looming deadlines? It could be a machine or could be a set of humans. Regardless, it's not impossible that coding on an object-oriented code base is easier or more difficult.

7.4 Exercises

1. True or False.
    a. Classes are easier to diagram than objects.
    b. Objects have more attributes than classes.
    c. Classes and objects are the same thing. They can be used interchangeably.
    d. Objects can be instantiated.
    e. Classes can be instantiated.
    f. A set of objects are called classes.
    g. A class can only create one instance of an object.

2. Describe inheritance to your grandparents.

3. Describe encapsulation to a 10-year-old child.

4. What is polymorphism?

5. What is the difference between method overloading and method overriding?

6. Name 3 more examples of information hiding and state why.

7. Real world modeling is one methodology used to model your design. As you saw, it translates pretty well into UML class diagrams.
    a. Use the real-world modeling method to draw the UML class diagram of the human body. Start with the head, limbs, and physical attributes.
    b. Use the real-world modeling method to draw the UML class diagram of a computer keyboard.
    c. Use the real-world modeling method to draw the UML class diagram of a simple chair.

8. What do you think could be some other criticisms of OOP? Name one and write how you would get around it. Extra credit: Name 3 and show how you would get around them.

[This page left intentionally blank]

8 POWER PRINCIPLES OF DESIGN

While there is definitely a science to designing objects, there is some art as well. Computer scientists and engineers have studied the best practices of designing objects and classes and have created a plethora of design principles to help guide us when we experience a design problem. Yes, the sheer number of design principles can be overwhelming, but we don't need to learn every single new design principle; we only need to learn the important concepts, and from there we could better understand existing design principles, and even derive our own if needed.

POWER Principles is a derivation of those important concepts as they are grounded in generalization (or abstraction) of computer science fundamentals. Unlike the more popular design principles like GRASP or SOLID, which at the surface appear to be similar to each other, POWER Principles takes a higher conceptual approach by looking at a class from all sides and from different lenses.

As our understanding of analysis and design have solidified, it's time we move on to understanding design principles. Before we learn POWER Principles!), we need to understand **why** you need to learn design principles in the first place!

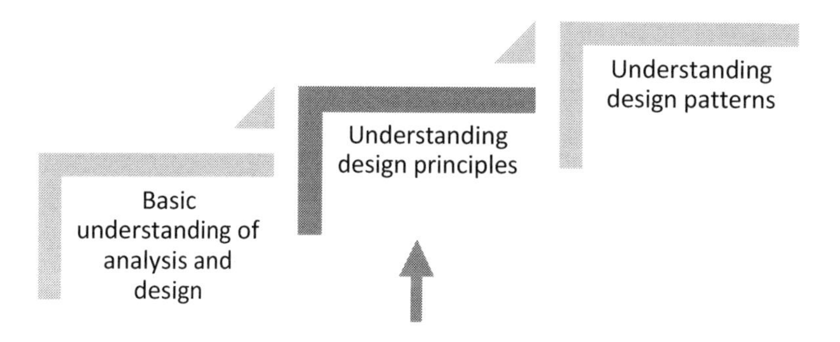

Why do you need to learn Object Oriented Design Principles?

Recall, the most important job we do as engineers is to satisfy the requirements laid before us. We need to do the job. We need to make sure the outputs of what we build matches the expected output. There is no other more important job.

However, if you want to come back to the code one day and enhance it, collaborate with others on it, maintain it, organize it, document it, or whatever you need to do with it, the problems of keeping code maintainable, extensible, and modular will eat you alive. The issues are compounded by the fact that you have many people working on the code base simultaneously from all parts of the world and in different time zones checking in and shipping code almost every hour of the day. **The machine, as we call the code, keeps changing non-stop like an amorphous being consuming those engineers alive who can't navigate the spaghetti procedural structure or seek peace behind a wall of abstraction.**

This is why we are studying the object oriented paradigm and this is the reason why object oriented exists in the first place. Recall, OO is about modeling the software in responsibilities, behaviors, and classes so that we humans can understand it better because it's the way the human brain has learned to understand things by compartmentalizing ideas and concepts into buckets. These buckets are what we call classes in the object oriented world.

On the contrary, you may be thinking that OO is not the only way to model software; there may be better ways. And you may be right, but it hasn't been proven yet. OO borrows concepts from real world modeling as we understand it better because it is similar to the real world where things are more relatable and tangible. There are many other ways as well and the design principles espoused by various computer scientists are some of those other ways.

Consequently, OO was created to address the 3 main issues of maintainability, extensibility, and modularity. But it wasn't enough. OO is like a knife, and it needs to be sharpened, honed, and handled the right way. The skill lies not in the knife itself, but lies within the person holding the knife to perform those actions.

Those skills are the design principles. And there are many of them. Fortunately, I've distilled them down into the POWER Principles.

8.1 The POWER Principles Overview

The POWER Principles is an object-oriented design framework that emphasizes generalizations and abstractions over detailed instructions. The reasons why POWER Principles were created are that given any problem that you as a software engineer would need to solve, it's best to be able to first identify the problem, think about the problem clearly, and then come up with your own solution rather than relying on predetermined solutions to match your problem. This framework or mindset is contrarian where traditionally, design principles are laid out in detail before you and you make sure your system does not violate any of them.

Ultimately, it doesn't matter at the end of the day if you are using Principle X or Principle Y to solve your problem, what matters is that the solution that you came up with solves the problem you are facing.

In OOAD, regardless of the framework (GRASP, SOLID, etc) the problems you face when designing classes are the following:

- How do I assign attributes? How do I assign methods?
- Where does this belong? How do I protect it?
- How do other modules use this? How do I maximize reuse?

Lastly, you want to know how well your design is performing.

- How is my design? Is it good? Bad? How efficient is my design?

Here's an illustration of the POWER Principles Framework:

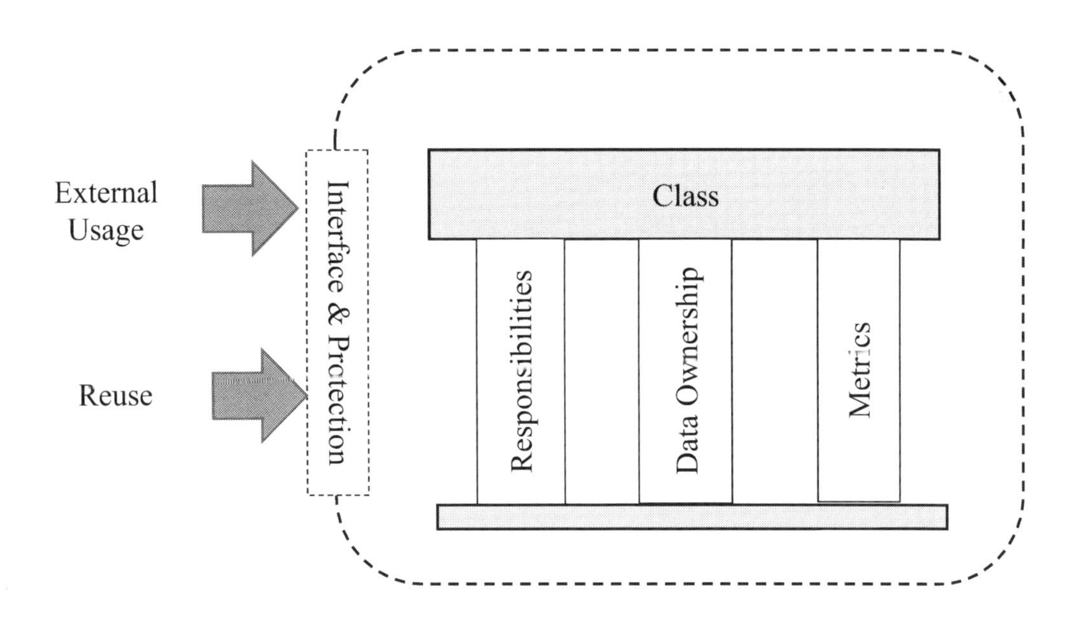

Imagine that you are building a house. You need to support it with a strong foundation and materials to build up the skeleton of the house. You need to add a roof and walls to protect the house and to decorate what the house looks like. You add doors and windows for people, air, and light to enter and exit. Once in a while, you need to make sure your house is not falling apart so you inspect it from time to time; you check the ceiling, faucets, and pipes to see if there are any leaks and you check the foundation for any cracks. When you find an issue, you repair it by patching it up or replacing the part. Then few years down the road, someone will approach you and say, "Hey, I like your house, can I build a replica?" You are flattered and so you provide them the blueprints to your house. They decide to borrow as much as possible, but tailor some aspects to their tastes.

Creating a class and determining what goes where in a system is the same analogy. Its data and behaviors determine the responsibilities it should have; this is analogous to the skeleton, roof, walls, and foundation of the house. Its interfaces or relationships to interfaces determine what others can do to it; this is analogous to the doors and windows. Regularly, you will want to inspect how your class did and you can look at the bugs found, lines of code for complexity, and other metrics; this is analogous to performing a regular inspection on your house. Finally, you want to make sure other modules can reuse your code either through inheriting or abstracting some of the concepts.

The POWER Principles were created through the lens of the diagram above.

By centering yourself as the home builder, owner, and altruistic designer of the house, you begin to view things with a lens that should make the house better over time. So putting this all together, in the diagram, the "Class" is held up by the 3 pillars: Responsibilities, Data Ownership, and Metrics. These three pillars provide the foundation of the Class and we will expound on each of them. Surrounding the Class is the Interface and Protection. Using the Interface are external classes and modules which may decide to simply call exposed methods or reuse logic. The interfaces are like the windows and doors to our Class.

8.2 The POWER Principles

The goals of the POWER Principles are:

- Guide you to design better classes by helping you think where attributes or methods should go
- Guide you to design better classes by helping you think what a single class should do or not do
- Guide you to design better classes by helping you think how classes should be exposed, and finally
- Guide you to design better classes by helping you think what constitutes an efficient class

The POWER Principles are the following:

- SINGLE RESPONSIBILITY
- DATA OWNERSHIP AND CREATION
- EXPOSITION VIA CONTRACTUAL INTERFACES
- EFFICIENCY METRICS

8.2.1 Single Responsibility

SINGLE RESPONSIBILITY means each class should have a single responsibility; or each class should be responsible for only one thing. This doesn't mean that a class should only have one method, instead, it means that *conceptually* a class should be responsible for one idea or concept.

Example #1: If you are defining a class on a concept called "AdditionProblems" and its responsibilities are to "generate a list of addition problems" and "print them into a PDF format", this class should ideally be split into two different classes because it does two completely different functions.

Why? You don't want to couple the two responsibilities together in one class. Instead, the generation of the problems and the printing of the problems should ideally be two separate activities. If you change the type of addition problems, say from 2 digit adding to 3 digits, you would most likely need to change the printing function or otherwise you'd have code that doesn't work! But if there were two separate classes (i.e. GenerateAdditionProblems and PrintAdditionProblems), the one thing common between them is an interface that specifies what kind(s) of problems that are allowed to be printed, so when the type of problems are changed, it becomes well known what else needs to be changed (if any) in the PrintAdditionProblems class.

The key here is the defined interface across classes, not within the class. You can also generalize the PrintAdditionProblems into a PrintProblems class so that it could print addition or subtraction questions as well. But you wouldn't be able to do that if you coupled both functions in one class. Thus, the need to be "modular" and bounded by an "interface" are the compelling reasons why a single class should have a single responsibility.

Example #2: Let's use a slightly different example. Imagine we have a general class called Car. It represents all the cars attributes and methods all in one class as follows:

```
class Car {
   int horsepower;
   int number_of_seats;
   Color color;

   public boolean startEngine(){..}
   public Boolean accelerate() {..}
   public Boolean decelerate() {..}
   public void turnOffEnginer() {..}
   public void openDoor(whichOne) {..}

}
```

The Car class does a lot of things! It seems to be responsible for the movement of the car as well as how the doors function. In fact, we say that this class would violate the Single Responsibility principle because it seems like every single method and attribute is at the "top level" in the class. How do we correct this? One way we can correct this is to split up the class into its responsibilities.

```
class Car {

   int number_of_seats;
   Color color;
   Engine car_engine;

   public void openDoor(whichOne)
   {..}

}
```

```
class Engine {

   int horsepower;

   public boolean startEngine(){..}
   public Boolean accelerate() {..}
   public Boolean decelerate() {..}
   public void turnOffEnginer() {..}

}
```

If we take out the "engine" components and isolate them into its own class, you will see that we have defined a set of responsibilities that the engine should do and belong to the engine. We've created an attribute in Car with an Engine type called car_engine so that it represents what kind of engine the car has. This isolates the Car to focusing on, for example, opening doors, while Engine focuses on engine related activities. (You can further break down this example and create a Door class. Exercise is left to the reader.)

Is SRP (Single Responsibility Principle) related to Responsibility Driven Design?

First, we need to define what is "Responsibility Driven Design" (or RDD). RDD is a design methodology that focuses on dividing the system into behaviors. This means that the resulting design is a collection of interacting processes where each process plays a specific and separate role from each other.

When you look at the UML class diagram of a system using RDD, you will find classes usually named with verbs such as "XYZ"-processor, "ABC"-controller, "DEF"-manager, etc. This means that the classes are behavior driven and they serve a functional purpose because they play the role of a do-er.

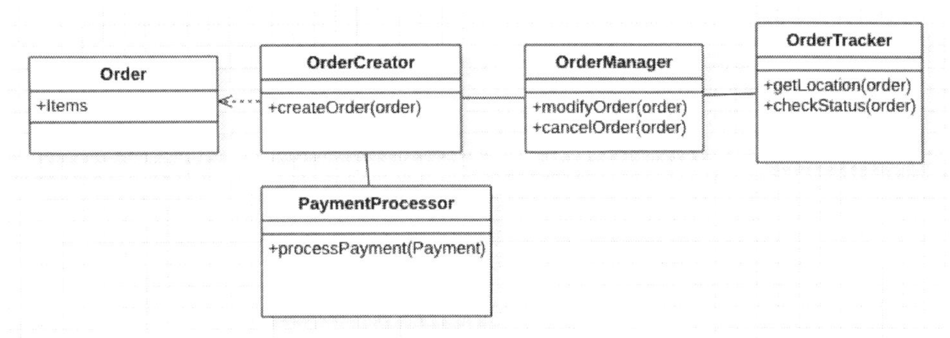

In the diagram above (which is a snippet from a much larger diagram), you see 4 classes with very specific behaviors/roles and serve an important function in the entire ordering process.

So, is RDD related to SRP? Yes, SRP is not exclusive to just RDD and they are not the same thing. SRP is a principle that is agnostic to design methodology. SRP generally says that each class (or module) that you create much have a single responsibility – it must do that one thing and do it very well. Each of the classes in the diagram above does their jobs. OrderManager, for example, does one thing, which is manages the order, and that entails allowing modifications to the order and cancelling the order, as two examples. Likewise, OrderTracker tracks the order and provides two methods that gets the location and checks the status of the order – both methods that aptly fall into the order tracking role.

How is Responsibility Driven Design different than Data Driven Design?

Data Drive Design (DDD) is different than RDD. In DDD, the focus is on dividing the system into objects that encapsulates the data. This is in stark contrast to RDD, where the focus is on dividing the system into separate behaviors. DDD is data-centric.

When you look at the UML class diagram of a system using DDD, you will find classes usually named with nouns such as Order, Payment, Person, etc. This means that the classes are data driven, because what forms the class is the encapsulation (or wrapper) of that data. So then where do the behaviors go? They are methods in the class. Let's see the same example as above, but using DDD.

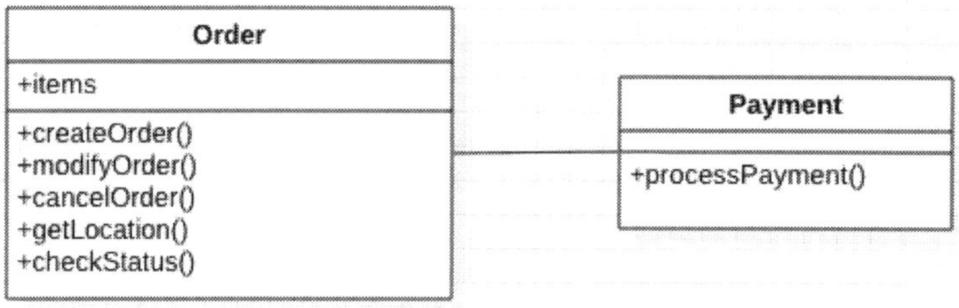

Order
+items
+createOrder()
+modifyOrder()
+cancelOrder()
+getLocation()
+checkStatus()

Payment
+processPayment()

In the diagram above (which is a snippet from a much larger diagram), you see only 2 classes – Order and Payment. They each encapsulate their own data and thus able to expose the methods that pertain to its data.

SRP is still related to DDD as SRP is not exclusive to any design methodologies. DDD is an application of SRP, just like RDD is an application of SRP. SRP only says that each class or module is responsible, and in the DDD case, Order class becomes a much larger class because it owns its data and thereby its methods.

I'm confused when to use Data Driven Design or Responsibility Driven Design. Please help!
Now, you may be wondering, DDD or RDD? Which way is "better"? When do I use each? This is a much more difficult question to answer, one that you have to decide yourself – but let me lay out the facts for you to make your decision easier (or not easier).

	PROs	CONs
DDD	• All the data is in one place. • The classes are broken up into concepts (nouns) that we all understand, which makes navigating the code easier.	• High Cohesion (discussed next section) may be harder to achieve given that all the behaviors are encapsulated in one class. • Behavior is sometimes difficult to navigate because you have to find the method associated with it, instead of first finding the behavioral class and then the methods. • Potentially super long classes in terms of lines of code
RDD	• High Cohesion is usually satisfied because the classes are behavioral centered. • Uses fewer lines of code per class • For some people, they think in actions rather than nouns, so this methodology may be more intuitive for them.	• Because the data may be interspersed, it may become difficult to navigate the various classes.

Is SRP (Single Responsibility Principle) related to High Cohesion Design Principle?

It's similar. A class that exhibits **low** cohesion is a class that has many responsibilities. Therefore, we want the opposite, High Cohesion, which is one of the GRASP Principles.

```
/* LOW COHESION */

class Apple {
      X
      Y
      methodX () {
            uses X
      }
      methodY () {
            usesY
      }
}
```

Therefore, we ideally want classes to show "High Cohesion" or methods that uses its own attributes/methods as extensively as possible so that it doesn't look like the method operates independently. Usually, highly cohesive classes exhibit single responsibility principle.

In the example to the right, class Apple exhibits low cohesion because its methods work independently of each other. methodX only uses variable X. methodY only uses variable Y. There is no "cohesiveness" or togetherness. You could have a better design by splitting them into separate classes or have the existing methods make more use of the attributes or other methods.

How do we make this more cohesive? Below are two options that satisfy the high cohesion principle. In option #1, we could make the methods use one or two of the attributes (or even other methods within the class) so that the methods and attributes are not working too independently of each other. In Option #2, we split the classes into single responsibilities. Either of these options are two of many other valid solutions.

```
/* HIGH COHESION - OPTION 1*/

class Orange {
      X
      Y

      methodX () {
            uses X and Y
      }
      methodY () {
            uses X and Y
      }
}
```

```
/* HIGH COHESION - OPTION 2*/

class OrangeX {
      X
      methodX () {
            uses X
      }
}

class OrangeY {
      Y
      methodY () {
            uses Y
      }
}
```

Is SRP (Single Responsibility Principle) related to Low Coupling Design Principle?

Low Coupling (one of the GRASP Principles) means that two have code that minimize dependencies on each other. A side effect of solving for low coupling is that the resulting classes could exhibit single responsibility principle.

Here's how: Low Coupling addresses the problem of modifying the code in the future, and so if you were to do so, how do you minimize impact to the original design? If the code had single responsibility in the first place, then impact is usually less. But if it's not, then impact would be high.

```
/* HIGH COUPLING EXAMPLE */

class A {
        fooA
        barA
        methodA{
                uses B.fooB directly
        }
        method2 {
                uses B.method directly
        }
}

class B {
        fooB
        barB
        methodB {
                uses A.fooA directly
        }
}
```

Let's go deeper. Let's look at an example of High Coupling (what we don't want for modularity and maintainability) to the right.

So, what's going on in the example?

- Class A's methodA uses class B's fooB attribute.
- Class A's method2 uses class B's methodB.
- Class B's methodB uses class A's fooA attribute.

It looks like we have a tangled web of calls that are interdependent. This makes the code hard to read and difficult to debug. This also makes the two classes very dependent on each other.

Creating classes that depend on each other is allowed, but it's frowned upon because it shows high coupling. So, if you want to de-couple the interdependencies, then you will make the code easier to read and more independent of each other. And when you split up the code, you will have code that is responsible for its own properties and have fewer calls creating interdependencies.

How do we resolve this?

A solution is to the right. What if you moved the methods to where they belong? Thereby solidifying the class to do what it should be doing with its attributes and/or methods?

```
/* LOW COUPLING SOLUTION */

class A {
        fooA
        barA

        method2 {
                uses B.method directly
        }
        methodB {
                uses A.fooA directly
        }
}

class B {
        fooB
        barB
        methodA{
                uses B.fooB directly
        }
}
```

So, we moved methodB to class A and methodA to class B. We kept the attributes where (we think) they belong. This solution means that there is no longer any interdependency among the two classes. In fact, they operate as pretty independent classes. Low coupling does not mean to make them independent, it just means that we want to avoid cyclical interdependencies or two-way relationships as much as possible.

8.2.2 Data Ownership & Creation Design Principle

DATA OWNERSHIP AND CREATION (DOC) means that if the class has the information then that class is responsible for the processing of it and exposing or not exposing it.

Example #1: If you are defining a class on a concept called "SubtractionProblem" which represents one single subtraction equation. In order to subtract the class, it needs two numbers called subtrahend (first number) and minuend (second number). Those numbers are attributes of the class, or said differently, the class is responsible for those numbers because it has the information.

SubtractionProblem
+subtahend +minuend

Now, where should you as the designer of the SubtractionProblem class place the difference (result)? Would you put it as an attribute in the class? A method that you'd always have to compute? Or would you put it somewhere outside the class because you don't think it belongs there? The answer (literally) is that the difference should reside within the class because the SubtractionProblem class owns the result of the operation; it shouldn't belong anywhere else. It has the numbers to compute it, not some other class, and because it has the information/data to do it, then it should own it.

Example #2: Using the same example #1 with SubtractionProblem, imagine we have a method called "getAnswer()" that returns the difference of the subtrahend and minuend. This method is located within the class as we discussed in Example #1. Should we expose this method externally meaning that anyone outside the class can call it or keep the method only for calls internal to the class? The answer is that there is no right answer; it really depends on what you want to do with it. You can expose it so that other modules can reuse it. Or you can hide it and decide to precompute the difference and store that as an attribute or not. The choice is yours because that class owns its data and it gets to decide what to do with that piece of data.

SubtractionProblem
+subtahend +minuend
-getAnswer()

Example #3: Imagine you are designing a retail store and you have decided to create a class called OrderManagement, which places the customer's orders. It has a helper class called OrderList that keeps track of all the orders. There is also another important class called ShoppingCart which stores the items in the customer's shopping cart. Now here's the question: In which class should the Order instances be created?

The answer is as follow: if it has the information then it should create it. Well, ShoppingCart has the information, should it create it? ShoppingCart only holds the items, but it doesn't contain whose shopping cart it is and the payment methodology for the order. Could it be OrderList? No, OrderList only keeps track of the orders and so is not in a position to create Order instances. We are left with OrderManagement. OrderManagement would effectively need to create an order based on the information in ShoppingCart (so there is a dependency there) and other classes as well. It would need to take in information about the Customer (assuming there is a Customer class) and Payments (assuming there is some type of payment class so we can get the details). OrderManagement serves as an aggregator of information and because it itself might not have all the information, it goes and gets it to achieve its responsibilities. No other class should create Orders because Payment's job is only payments, and Customer class is only for customer information.

Is DOC related to Information Expert Principle?

The Information expert principle, one of the GRASP principles, applies mainly to the attributes and methods of a class. The principle states that "if the class has the information necessary to fulfill it, then that class should be assigned the responsibility of the information expert."[9]

I tend to use a different and more straightforward definition: If the information belongs to the class, then it is the information expert and it should fulfill its role as information expert by adding the corresponding attributes and/or methods. So, if you own the information, then you are the information expert.

Is DOC related to Creator Design Principle?

The Creator principle (which is one of the GRASP Principles) assigns the responsibility of creation of an instance of another object if any of the following conditions are met. So, for example, we would assign class B the responsibility of creator of class A, if any of the following conditions are met.

- Instances of B contains or aggregates instances of A.
- Instances of B has the data to create instances of A.
- Instances of B records instances of A.
- Instances of B closely uses A.

The creator principle is pretty straightforward. Essentially, if you have the data to create instances of A, then you are the creator; if you have a job of containing or recording or aggregating instances of A, then you are the creator; and finally, if you extensively use instance A, then you are the creator.

For those craving for more advanced design patterns, this Creator principle is synonymous with the Factory pattern. The Factory pattern allows you to create an object without exposing the creation logic. This is done by using a common interface called a Factory class that allows the caller (or client) to get instances of the class in a common way. If you have seen code such as XYZFactory class, you'll see that the sole purpose of the code is to churn out instances of one or more types.

---

[9] Larman, Applied UML and Patterns, 3rd Edition.

Here is a code sample (without error checking) that illustrates a Factory pattern.

```
interface Weird {
}

class Foo implements Weird {
}

class Bar implements Weird {
}

class Baz implements Weird {
}
```

```
class WeirdFactory {
   public Weird getWeird(String type)
   {
      if type.equals("Foo")
         return new Foo();
      if type.equals("Bar")
         return new Bar();
      if type.equals("Square")
         return new Square();
   }
}
```

The WeirdFactory is the Factory class that returns instances of Weird types. The Weird types are Foo, Bar, and Baz, which are of type Weird. To use the Weird Factory class, you would do this:

```
WeirdFactory wf = new WeirdFactory();
Foo f = wf.getWeird("Foo");
Bar b = wf.getWeird("Bar");
Baz z = wf.getWeird("Baz");
```

We would say that WeirdFactory exhibits the Creator principle since it creates the objects (and also exhibits the Factory design pattern).

8.2.3 EXPOSITION VIA CONTRACTS & INTERFACES DESIGN PRINCIPLE

EXPOSITION VIA CONTRACTS & INTERFACES (EVCAI) says that the designer of the class should determine whether to expose its attributes and/or methods when working on a system with many modules. This exposition is called an interface of a class and becomes a contract that other classes understand and make use of.

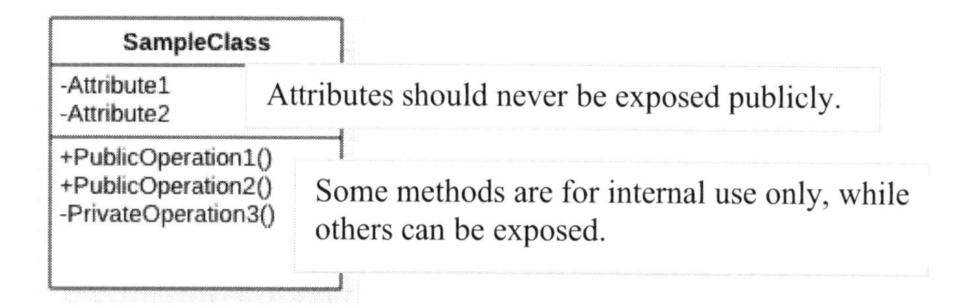

In the SampleClass above, attributes should almost always never be exposed publicly. Why? You may want to regulate how other classes use the attribute. Say you want to only allow read operations on the attribute, so a solution is to create a getter method: getAttribute1(). Or you only want to allow write operations, so a solution is to create a setter method: setAttribute1(value). You as the designer define what to expose and what not to expose.
What you expose then becomes the contractual interface.

What SampleClass sees	What other Classes See
SampleClass -Attribute1 -Attribute2 +PublicOperation1() +PublicOperation2() -PrivateOperation3()	SampleClass +PublicOperation1() +PublicOperation2()

Why is a contractual interface important?
A contractual interface defines what the consuming class can and cannot do with the subject class.

It also specifies what could be available. This is important when you work in distributed teams. Imagine you have team A working on a checkout feature of your e-commerce store and team B working on a feature to add payment in order to checkout. Both teams must work in parallel or otherwise they won't meet the deadline. So, what do they do? TeamB can create an interface and say "OK team A, these are the methods that you can call to process the payment when you checkout. They don't work yet, but the method signatures won't change or if they do, it'll be minor. So, you won't be able to test it yet until we let you know it works, but we are not blocking your development as you have other work to do". How's that for an answer? Both teams are not blocked and can proceed their owns ways independently.

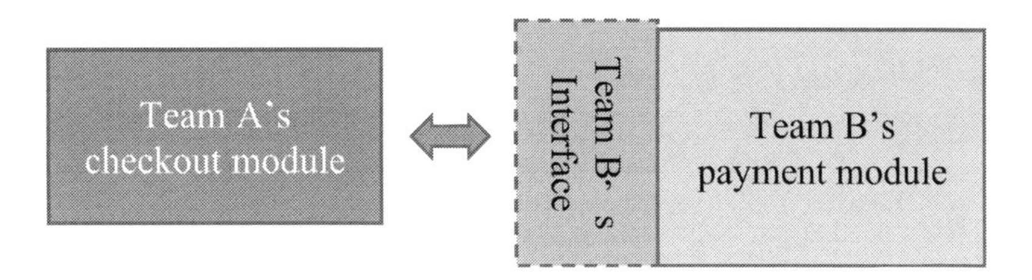

Is EVCAI related to Protected Variations Design Principle?

Protected Variations (one of the GRASP Principles) is the identification of "points of predicted variation or instability and assign responsibilities to create a stable interface around them"[10]. Or said more simply: Wrap the class in an interface so that it resolves ambiguity or issues.

There is essentially one main way to wrap a class: via polymorphism. We specify an interface class and then we create subclasses from the interface class. This interface class is what we can share with other teams as the contractual interface. Our subclasses, which could also be interfaces, would need to implement the methods specified in the interface. By being careful about what to expose, we satisfy the principle of protected variation.

Is EVCAI related to Open/Closed Principle?

The Open/Closed Principle (one of the SOLID Principles) states that "software entities should be open for extension but closed for modification". This is achieved only through generalization (i.e. inheritance).

A class is "open" meaning that another class can extend it. When you extend it, you make it a parent or superclass. That means you are free to overwrite or override any of the methods.

A class is "closed" meaning that another class cannot change or modify its code. The original class (which all classes should be closed) is not open for modification and will never be even when the other class inherit from it, the original class' code never changes. We say that the original class is "protected" from modification.

So only when you extend it in the open principle, you can modify its interface of methods in the new class if needed.

[10] Larman, Applying UML and Patterns, 3rd Edition.

Is EVCAI related to Interface Segregation Principle?

The Interface Segregation Principle (ISP), one of the SOLID Principles states that "no clients should be forced to depend on methods it does not use"[11]. This means as a designer of the original interface, you may consider splitting the interface into separate components so that each interface's responsibilities are isolated from other irrelevant responsibilities. So, an interface for Engine should only expose methods that control, manage, and provide status of the engine instance; it shouldn't also provide methods that open/close doors or sunroofs. So, a client can pick and choose which interfaces (Engine interface or Door interface) to complete its work.

This idea is similar and goes back to the Single Responsibility Principle. An interface, just like a class, should provide a coherent set of responsibilities.

Is EVCAI related to Encapsulation?

Yes. Encapsulation is the hiding or restricting of the object's attributes and methods. By setting them to "public" or "private" or any other state offered by the programming language of choice, the class can achieve unauthorized access. Another terminology that is used is called "Information hiding".

As an example, in SuperSecret class below, we only allow getting the SSN, but we don't allow setting it. Using getters and setters, we can control what others can do with the data.

Is EVCAI related to Abstraction?

Yes and No. Abstraction as a term has been severely overloaded[12], so let's clear the confusion.

Abstraction is a process used to solve computer science problems by not focusing on low level details but the higher order bits. As an example, when you are first learning computer science, you learned the concept of recursion. It was an abstract topic because you had to convince yourself that it would work – that by solving the higher order problem (the n-1 problem), the recursion process would eventually solve the entire problem. This leap of faith by focusing on the higher-level problem is called abstraction. When we say we can solve a problem via "abstraction", we say that we will focus on the higher order bit and solve the higher-level problem.

Another example of abstraction is the layer or interface between software and hardware. When the hardware changes, you don't have to rewrite your application because the operating system abstracts the hardware from your application. It is the operating system's job to hide details about the hardware so that it doesn't affect the applications that run on the operating system. Therefore, the operating system is a form of abstraction.

---

[11] SOLID Principles, Wikipedia.org

[12] http://www.tonymarston.co.uk/php-mysql/abstraction.txt

Similarly, in object-oriented design, abstraction is the separation of the implementation and the interface. It masks or hides the background details so that the client using the interface is not concerned about how it works but that it does work.

So how is abstraction related to EVCAI? The relationship is subtle because the interface that the class exposes hides the details about how the methods work – all we need to know as clients of the interface is that it will do its job.

What is the difference between Encapsulation and Abstraction?

The pictures below illustrate the difference between Abstraction and Encapsulation.

Abstraction, as we stated before, is the process or layer where you show what you need to show and hide all the unnecessary details. The diagram on the left is a picture of a calculator. We say that is a form of abstraction because all you need to know as a user is to press buttons and the calculator will do its work and give you the answer. You don't have to worry about all the nitty gritty details that go on inside.

Encapsulation, as we discussed in the previous chapters and sections, is the process of combining the relevant data and methods into modules or classes so that they may exhibit single responsibility behavior. In the diagram to the right, we show an exploded view of the internals of the calculator and its internal modules. Each of those modules is an encapsulation of data and responsibilities. They work together by exposing the right amount of data so that they can operate together as a calculator. For example, the Button Sensor module would most likely expose a method called "buttonPressed(Button)" so that the 12 Buttons module can trigger it. But Button Sensor module would never expose a method called "callCPU()" because doing so would violate its responsibilities (it doesn't have the right to create that method, only CPU would). Instead, inside Button Sensors, there is a private method that makes the call to the CPU to compute the input provided by the user.

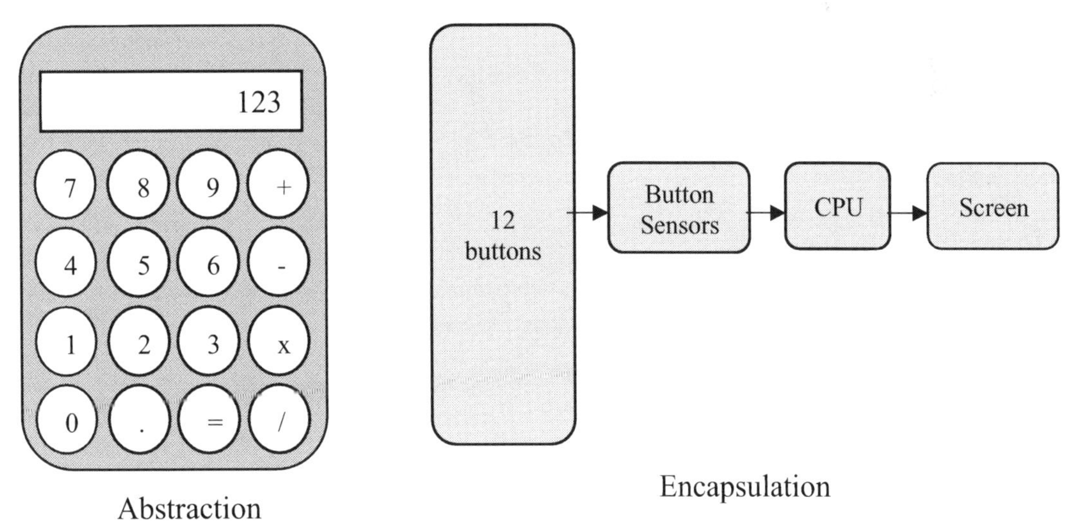

Abstraction

Encapsulation

8.2.4 EFFICIENT POWER METRIC

The final POWER Principle is the POWER metric, which are a set of questions and guidelines to make you think whether you are designing the class and other related classes in an *efficient* object-oriented manner.

So, what makes a class or your design *efficient*?

> An **efficient class** is a class that can stand the test of time; it is immediately understandable by name, by function, by behavior; it is short in terms of lines of code because a large class takes up more computer memory and makes it difficult for engineers to decipher; and finally, it is organized and documented adequately so engineers can quickly go into the class, make the modifications or fixes, and move on.
>
> An **efficient system** is a collection of efficient classes. If every single class is efficient, then the entire system is efficient. Additionally, an efficient system is a system where interfaces between classes and interfaces between external and internal systems are well-defined so that an outsider determining how to use a class or how to use the system is not a laborious or confusing chore.

Let's use the following metrics to define efficiency in our classes and systems:

- Time it takes for an engineer to fix what your team deems as a "small t-shirt size" bug
- Time it takes for an engineer to complete what your team deems as a "small t-shirt size" task
- How descriptive is the class name.
- Number of cycles if you were only to draw a UML class diagram using the Dependency Association.
- The number of lines of code of a specific class
- The total average lines of code of the system per class.
- Number of interfaces used relative to the number of classes

Time it takes for ...
The time-it-takes metric is a difficult one to obtain and only obtainable after the class is in production, as in the code has shipped to customers. So, trying to get data for this metric before the code is released would not be feasible. This means that in order for you to determine if this class is efficient, you would only be able to determine the time while the code is in production. may need to refactor the code if any undesirable inefficiencies are found.

Example: The ice cream machine has a bug where every time the customer orders strawberry flavored ice cream, only mango ice cream comes out. But when a customer orders mango ice cream, they get mango. Your team has decided that this is a small t-shirt size bug, meaning that it would probably take an average engineer about 1 day to fix the issue. Assume you are an average engineer and you end up taking 3 days because you couldn't find the piece of buggy code; it wasn't in the Strawberry class or the Inventory Manager class. In fact, the bug was somehow in the OrderScreen class. We say that the class (and system) is inefficient because it took you more time than necessary because the code was not readily understandable and it appears some code was in the wrong place!

Descriptive Class Name

Coming up with a descriptive class name is an art. You want a name that is not too long but not too short. You want a name that immediately tells the engineer "this is what this class is. Period." Here are some examples of class names that are descriptive (and yes, you may discover that Responsibility Driven Design classes hold more descriptive names", but you may also discover that it may be more difficult to find given the number of classes you would have to read through).

Descriptive names generally follow this pattern: Adjective-Noun-Noun (where at least one of those nouns is the noun form of the verb).

Example #1: OrderProcessor

First noun is Order. Second noun is Processor, the noun form of Process.

Example #2: WeddingCoordinator

First noun is Wedding. Second noun is Coordinator, the noun form of Coordinate.

Example #3: SortedIntegerArray

First word is an adjective Sorted. Second is noun Integer. The third is noun Array.

Example #4: ReverseSortedIntegerQueue

First word is an adjective Reverse and second is adjective Sorted. Sorted is a highly descriptive word. Third word is noun Integer. The fourth is noun Queue.

Here are some examples of names that are not very descriptive:

- System (What kind of system? What does the system do?)
- Tool (Unless this is a super class, what kind of tool for what?)
- Just an adjective
    - Adjectives such as "Innovative" usually aren't very descriptive by itself. You will want to combine it with other words to make it better or not use the word at all due to ambiguity: But if you must use it, here's an example that even I balk at using: InnovativeStringQueue.
    - InnovativeCar (The adjective "innovative" isn't descriptive)
    - CoolObject (The adjective "cool" isn't descriptive, unless it's a name that everyone on the project already understands)
    - FastCar (Unless the name of the car is "FastCar", this is not a very descriptive name because all the other cars that you create could very well be considered "fast".)

Number of Cycles in Dependency UML Graph
Imagine you did a UML class diagram, but only used Dependency Association between the classes. In effect, you have just created a UML Class Dependency Graph.

The idea is to find cycles where classes call each other. If they call each other, they may be considered highly coupled, and that may be one reason for you to consider refactoring the code. As we have learned, code that

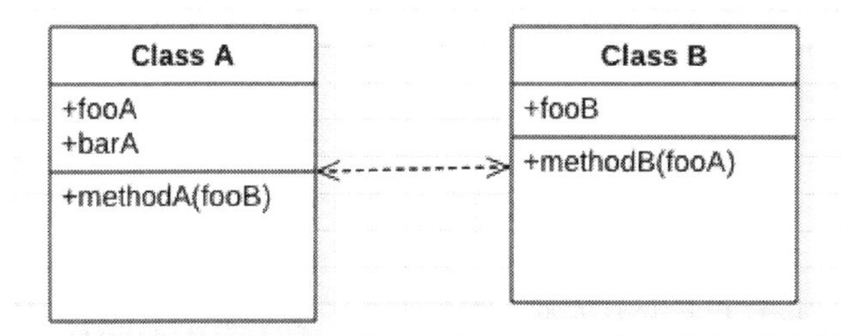

is highly coupled is inefficient because it would take time for an engineer to decipher the tangle web of calls when modifying or fixing a bug in the code.

Number of Lines of Code in a Class
One way to measure complexity is to look at the number of lines of code in a class. The idea is that the more lines of code a class contains, the more complex it is. It may even have become "bloated" to take on more behaviors or states than what was originally intended and therefore may violate the Single Responsibility Principle. Whatever the reason is, the number of lines of code is one or many indicators to tell the complexity and thereby efficiency of the class.

Ideally, you would want each class to be around 300 lines of code. Yes, this sounds super arbitrary and no line should be drawn that harshly. I've seen numbers of 250 or even lower. So, if you are starting to doubt the length of your class, you may want to investigate the class again to see if it as complicated as the number of lines of code makes it seem. However, I would not refactor the code just because the class has more than 300 lines; this needs to be a decision made with other inputs as well.

Average Number of Lines of Code in a System
If every class in the system adheres to a defined set of number of lines of code per class, then mathematically, the entire system, on average, adheres as well. It would be wise to look at this average number of lines of code per class to see if it's trending upwards. Historically, this number should almost always stay constant with some dips and highs but the trend should be flat over time. Now, if the trend is trending upwards, it would be good idea to see what's causing this. Did new classes get added over time? Were there new features added? Do the new features belong in that one class or should it be separated? Those are some of the questions that you can ask yourself if you start seeing things out of the ordinary.

Number of Interfaces in a System

One of the reasons why Amazon Web Services was so successful is that they built the services with "well documented APIs"[13] so that each service interfaced with each other via exposed sets of APIs. A service for databases exposed a set of APIs. A service for file storage exposed its set of APIs. A service for servers and computation exposed its set of own APIs. This allowed a common methodology for various services to talk to each other – APIs. We say that this system is efficient because published APIs that are well documented saves engineers time from helping each other and instead engineers can self-help their way to success.

So, for the system that you build, no matter how simple or complicated, could benefit from the methodology. If each class that you wrote had a well-documented interface, how easy would it be for some other team who you work with to take that interface and use it in their own code without asking you a single question?

[13] https://techcrunch.com/2016/07/02/andy-jassys-brief-history-of-the-genesis-of-aws/

8.2 POWER Principles Summary

If there is a one-liner takeaway about the POWER Principles, it would be "design the class as if you lived in it". Imagine that you are the class and you are designing that house. What does it look like? What does it own? What does it do? How do you protect it? How do you share it? How do you make sure it's always in livable condition?

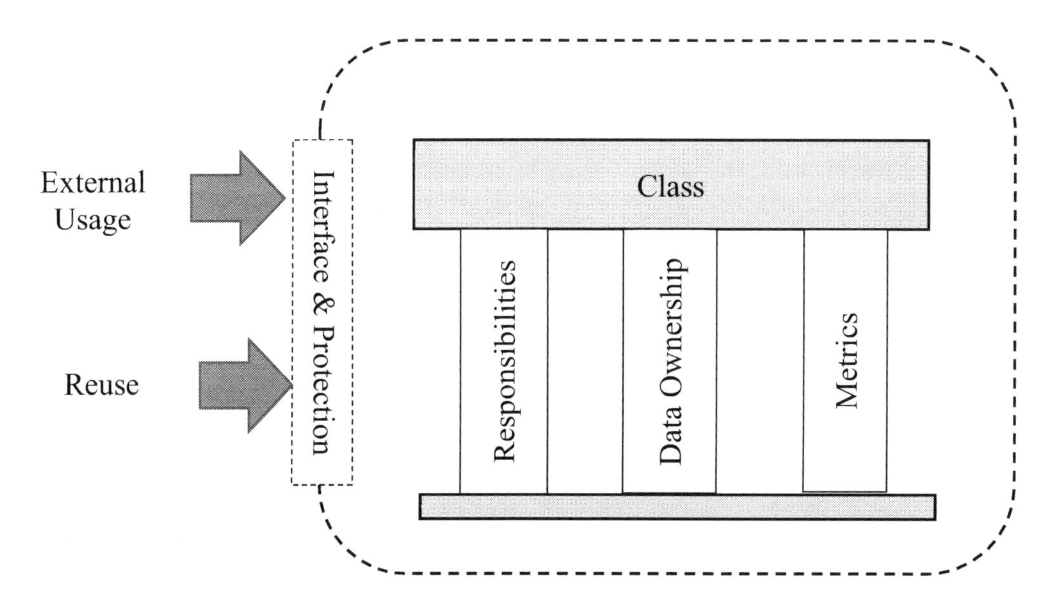

Recall, the goals of the POWER Principles are:

- Guide you to design better classes by helping you think where attributes or methods should go
- Guide you to design better classes by helping you think what a single class should do or not do
- Guide you to design better classes by helping you think how classes should be exposed, and finally
- Guide you to design better classes by helping you think what constitutes an efficient class (

The POWER Principles are the following:

- SINGLE RESPONSIBILITY
- OWNERSHIP AND CREATION
- EXPOSITION VIA CONTRACTUAL INTERFACES
- POWER EFFICIENCY METRIC

8.3 Exercises

1. What are the four POWER Principles?

2. Provide 3 examples of some descriptive class names.

3. Imagine that you are creating a ticketing system for buying movie tickets online. The most important use cases that your system must address is (1) allowing a customer to select which movie they want to buy ticket(s) for, (2) allowing customer to pay for the tickets using a credit card, (3) allowing customers to choose the type or tickets – kids, adults, or seniors, (4) allowing customers to cancel the tickets purchased.

   Use the ABCDG Method and then the POWER Principles to come up with a UML Class Diagram of your design. (You will need to make some assumptions. If you do, please document the assumptions taken).

4. Imagine that you are tasked with creating software that helps kids build simple robots. The most important use cases that your system must address is (1) kids will only be using a tablet computer, (2) kids can create a new design or work on an existing one, (3) kids can drag and drop pre-made functions such as "move forward/backward", "move backward", "turn left/right", "play a sound", "detect a human face", into a straight line to form a program that the robot must follow, and (4) kids can share the design with their friends on YouTube.

   Use the ABCDG Method and then the POWER Principles to come up with a UML Class Diagram of your design. (You will need to make some assumptions. If you do, please document the assumptions taken).

5. What are some other ways that you can measure the "efficiency" of an object-oriented class?

[This page left intentionally blank]

9 COMPARING DESIGN PRINCIPLES

In this chapter, we will compare POWER Principles to other design principles such as GRASP and SOLID. It will take some time for the POWER Principles to be as popular (if ever) as the other design principles. After all, almost all the other Design Principles in existence have had over a decade of exposure to students and professionals alike. Out of the many, many design principles out there, I'd like to provide a short comparison overview of GRASP and SOLID as they are the two more popular ones.

9.1 Comparing GRASP Design Principles

GRASP stands for General Responsibility Assignment Software Patterns (or Principles). It's a methodology, "a mindset", according to GRASP creator Craig Larman[14]. So, it's not technology and not UML. It's a little bit of Design Patterns as well as what the acronym implies. Regardless of what it may be, we can use GRASP to help shape our UML diagrams and help us be better designers. (On a side but important note, this book is not a complete overview of GRASP and the author urges the reader to read up on GRASP and other design principles in Larman's book or the many online resources).

GRASP has 9 principles and we will briefly compare them, although we've actually covered most of them in the POWER Principles chapter. By the way, there is no set order that you should review the 9 principles, but I think my ordering below will help you understand GRASP better.

[14] Please see the References section if you want to read more about GRASP in Larman's book.

GRASP Principle #1 – Controller

The first GRASP Principle that we will tackle is Controller.

The Controller's job is to coordinate and manage calls coming from within or external to the system.

The diagram below shows one example where a Controller would sit within the system due to its functions. In the example, the Controller coordinates the calls coming from the UI which ultimately gets processed by one of the sub-systems. Another way to look at this is a hub-and-spoke model, where the controller is the hub and the spokes are the various calls from the subsystems.

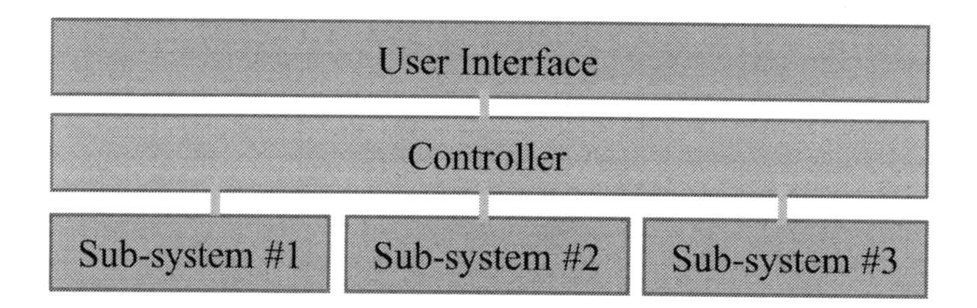

Another example is the Model-View-Controller Pattern (MVC). It is one of the most widely used patterns because it separates the responsibilities into three logical and separate components. As a result, one of the benefits is software engineers can develop in parallel and reuse code. Use of MVCs are with frameworks that are tied to a specific programming language such as Ruby on Rails, JavaScript, Python, PHP, Java, and many others. In MVC, the User of the system interacts with the Controller, which changes the Model. The Model changes updates the View, which in term updates what the User sees. The diagram below shoes the interactions.

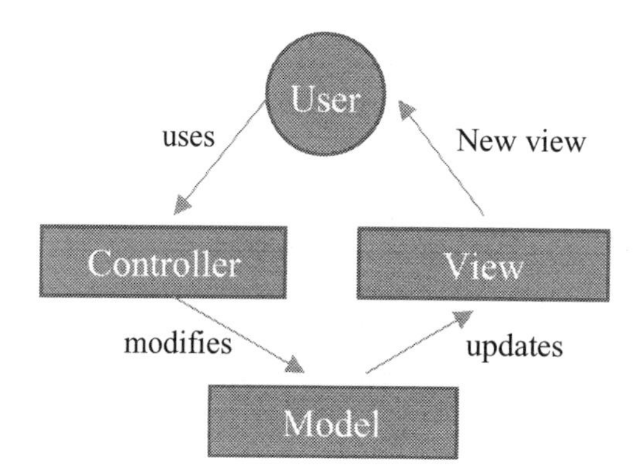

In the ICM example, which class most closely represented the Controller? (Hint: Order Screen. In ICM Order Screen serves both UI and Controller purposes. The way that we have architected ICM is not an example of MVC.)

GRASP Principle #2 – Creator

See example for Low Coupling in POWER Principles Data Ownership and Creator.

GRASP Principle #3 – Information Expert
See example for Low Coupling in POWER Principles Data Ownership and Creator.

GRASP Principle #4 – Low Coupling
See example for Low Coupling in POWER Principles Single Responsibility.

GRASP Principle #5 – High Cohesion
See example for High Cohesion in POWER Principles Single Responsibility.

GRASP Principle #6 – Indirection
See example for Abstraction in POWER Principles Exposition Via Abstraction and Contractual Interfaces.

GRASP Principle #7 – Polymorphism
See example for Polymorphism in POWER Principles Exposition Via Abstraction and Contractual Interfaces and Chapter 7.

GRASP Principle #8 – Pure Fabrication
The premise for this principle is like making a forced decision when picking between two or more evils. When you are trying to satisfy High Cohesion and Low Coupling or other goals, but your code doesn't allow it, how do would you get around it? Larman suggests instead of choosing one of the evils, you would be better off creating a new class, which is responsible for satisfying the principles you wish not to violate. This new "made up" (or fabricated) class solves the problem by not modifying any of the existing classes and moving the potentially violating logic from the class to the newly fabricated class.

Let's look at an example.

> Imagine you have an Order class and it holds the information for Orders. Orders would need to be saved to a database in order to persist the data. You have several evil options: (1) Build database saving logic into Orders, thereby coupling them both, or (2) Build database saving logic into Orders, thereby duplicating logic that may be in other classes, or (3) Build database saving logic into Orders, thereby violating cohesiveness because database operations don't naturally belong in Orders. You may argue that according to Information Expert (GRASP Principle #3) Order has the data and so it should be free to do as it pleases with that data. So, there are potentially three violations of the GRASP Principles and one object oriented basic violation of code reuse with just this simple example.
>
> However, there are actually multiple solutions, one of which uses indirection (abstraction) and another using Pure Fabrication. The pure fabrication solution creates a new class with the sole purpose of saving data into a database (and potentially other actions). If you have ever seen a static class before in Java with only static methods inside, it may be a use of pure fabrication. One of those methods could be saving order data into a database.
>
> The other cleaner solution is using abstraction and this goes back to the single responsibility principle. Although Orders has the data, it should not necessarily have that responsibility to save to database because others may want to reuse that same logic. So naturally, there should be a new responsibility to

just save data (regardless of what it is) to a database. This abstraction layer over the database would be a wise choice because it would hide the SQL code from Order and furthermore could use interfaces to separate what the database abstraction layer can and cannot do.

This is a case of deciding which design principle or computer science concept to use. Don't always take the design principles advertised by others to always be true or the answer to everything. There are multiple factors that go into a decision and sometimes, the simpler solution (i.e. abstraction) will win out.

GRASP Principle #9 – Protected Variation

See example for Protected Variation in POWER Principles Exposition Via Abstraction and Contractual Interfaces.

9.2 Comparing SOLID Principles

Similar to GRASP, SOLID offers a slightly different take of the object-oriented design principles. SOLID was created by Robert C. Martin[15]. (On a side note, this book does not provide a complete overview of SOLID and the author urges the reader to read upon SOLID principles in the many available resources including online).

There are 5 SOLID Principles, and we've actually compared most of them in the POWER Principles chapter, so now we'll cover the principles that we didn't get a chance to go over.

SOLID Principle #1 – Single Responsibility Principle

See POWER Principles Single Responsibility. The POWER Principles borrows from the Single Responsibility Principle and expands upon it conceptually.

SOLID Principle #2 – Open-Closed Principle

See example for Open-Closed Principle in POWER Principles Exposition Via Abstraction and Contractual Interfaces.

[15] https://en.wikipedia.org/wiki/Robert_C._Martin

SOLID Principle #3 – Liskov Substitution Principle

The Liskov Substitution Principle has a fancy name but don't let that scare you. It was created in 1987 by Barbara Liskov when she introduced behavioral subtyping at a conference[16]. Given the mathematics involved in the definition, here's the slimmed-down takeaway: When deciding to make a subclass, make sure that all its behaviors are consistent with what you want the subclass to be. Because if they are not, then the behavior cannot be substituted or swapped out.

An example of this is: Should a circle be a subclass of an oval?

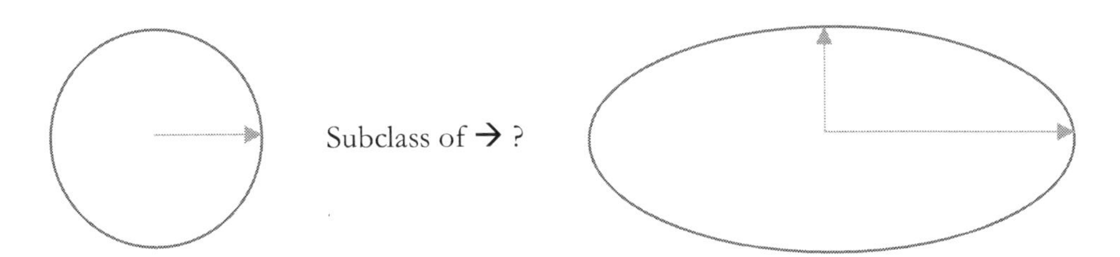

Example: If you have a Circle class and an Oval class, you being the object-oriented expert, would like to make one a subtype of another. After all, they look very similar! Specifically, you want Circle to be a subtype of Oval because Circle is just a special type of Oval as Circle has a consistent radius while Oval has two radii. So, in Oval, it is natural to have the two methods: setRadiusVertical and setRadiusHorizontal. But in Circle, you really only need to have one method which is setRadius. Liskov says you can't make the subclass more restrictive than the superclass. So, you can't technically make Circle a subclass of Oval because then you'd have to keep track and call both methods, which is not a direct substitution.

SOLID Principle #4 – Interface Segregation Principle

See example for Interface Segregation Principle in POWER Principles Exposition Via Abstraction and Contractual Interfaces.

SOLID Principle #5 – Dependency Inversion Principle

The Dependency Inversion Principle (DIP) states that both high level and low-level modules should depend on abstractions such as interfaces. DIP is a methodology for decoupling the relationship between two modules and this methodology is abstraction. So instead of the high level depending on low level, they each depend on the same abstraction.

Example: Imagine you have 3 classes: SmartStudent, SmarterStudent, and Teacher. Before DIP is applied, pretend that you have the following code:

[16] https://en.wikipedia.org/wiki/Liskov_substitution_principle

```
class SmartStudent {
   void takeTest() { .. }
}

class SmarterStudent {
   void takeTest() { .. }
}

class Teacher {
   SmartStudent julie;

   void popQuizTime() {
      julie.takeTest();
   }
}
```

Based on the above code, Teacher is only teaching the SmartStudent's, but not the SmarterStudents. How do we make Teacher also teach the SmarterStudents? You would need to do this:

```
class Teacher {
   SmartStudent julie;
   SmarterStudent jackie;

   void popQuizTime() {
      julie.takeTest();
      jackie.takeTest();
   }
}
```

In effect, you've tied the two Student classes together with Teacher, effectively coupling them. That violates the low coupling principle. So, what does DIP recommend?

Create a Student interface (see next page) so that Teacher can work on the Students more generally. This way, instead of the Teacher depending on the two types of Students directly, the Teacher depends on its abstraction which is the Student interface and the two types of Students also depend on the same Student interface.

In general, using interfaces is a common practice in software design and development. Having a contractual interface that can be shared across teams or even individuals is good practice. In fact, this harkens back to the more generalized POWER Principle in Exposition Via Abstraction and Contractual Interfaces.

```
interface Student {
   void takeTest();
}

class SmartStudent implements Student {
   void takeTest() { .. }
}

class SmarterStudent implements Student {
   void takeTest() { .. }
}

class Teacher {
   Student s;

   void popQuizTime() {
      s.takeTest();
   }
}
```

[This page left intentionally blank]

9.3 Exercises

1. If you had to choose to follow one design principle framework – GRASP or SOLID or POWER Principles – which one would you choose and why?

2. How would you compare the POWER and the GRASP principles?

3. How would you compare the POWER and SOLID principles?

4. Pick a domain (i.e. transportation, e-commerce, dining) and create an example for each of the GRASP Principles.

5. Pick a domain (i.e. transportation, e-commerce, dining) and create an example for each of the SOLID Principles.

[This page left intentionally blank]

10 AGILE & OOAD

A lot of books on Object Oriented Analysis and Design have focused on various software development methodologies to either explain OOAD in a better light or promote a certain way of conducting software development. As you can see, this book did neither.

OOAD, as we have said before, is independent of any software development methodologies. OOAD doesn't require you to sit in pairs and design/program together (i.e. Extreme Programming) nor does it require you to set up JIRA boards (JIRA is popular bug and feature tracking software from Atlassian) and manage them in an agile fashion. OOAD makes you think about the what and why in developing software; whereas the software development methodologies tell you a specific process of development that is akin to project management. To be clear (and as you have seen if you've read this book without skipping any chapters), OOAD is not project management, OOAD is the design thought process in thinking what are we building, why are we building it, and how we can build it. Thus, it's completely independent of any software development lifecycle methodology.[17]

With that said, there are certain software development methods that bring out the brilliance of OOAD, but even so (as this is literally the 100th time I'm saying this), OOAD can operate by itself or with almost any other software development methods.

10.1 Agile.

Because Agile is one of the most popular software development methodologies since the early 2000s and may continue to be popular in the next decade(s), many authors and promoters have tied Agile and OOAD together and sold many books. And because many books have been sold (a certain textbook that I used in my course), I feel that you should know about it, get exposed to it, and understand why.

[17] Some pundits may disagree and that's ok. In fact, OOAD existed long before Agile, so OOAD had been around for some time before some of the popular software development methodologies came to be popular practice.

10.2 The Agile Manifesto

Found Here the Agile Manifesto is a set of 12 principles designed to guide software developers around the world who choose to follow it how to go about "designing software". Notice that I have placed "designing software" in quotes because "designing software" in the Agile Manifesto context has a different meaning than the "designing software" that I've used throughout this book. I'd like for you to click on the link for the Agile Manifesto (if you are reading the eBook) or take a small detour to look at the Agile Manifesto and read all 12 principles.

Now that you are back from that small detour, my definition of "Designing Software" used in the OOAD context is the following: Analyzing the use cases and requirements so that we can come up with a flexible software design that satisfies said use case and requirements.
On the other hand, the Agile Manifesto definition of "Design Software" is the following and I paraphrase from the Manifesto: Principles of how we work together as a team, as a client of a customer in developing software, and the continuous self-reflection and monitoring so we do better as a team.
As you can see, OOAD and Agile are completely two different sets of topics. One is more team and process oriented (Agile) and the other is more purely design oriented (OOAD).

10.3 Agile Definitions and Process

We will now learn one way (of many ways) that we can cohesively tie OOAD to Agile. (In the next section, we will do the same to waterfall software development methodology). But first, let's explain to you the nitty gritty details of Agile because it's important to know. You can read more about the Agile development methodology on any website (and you will find that they all differ in definition in some way), or you can read the below for my version of Agile that I have had direct experience with:

- Agile is expressed in sprints.
- Each sprint is between 2 and 4 weeks. (One or the other, but not both).
    - Some teams that you work with may use a 4-week sprint and you may be using a 2-week sprint.
    - Each team's sprint may have a different start date than yours. You may start Sprint 123 on February 1st, but the other team that you depend on for a module may start their Sprint on February 8th. So, aligning sprints in a cross-functional team environment with many dependencies can be tricky.
- Each sprint has a set of engineers, project manager, and product manager. These people are called a "Squad". Other teams may also exist to describe a collection of people working on a sprint. A Squad has a name because in a large project, you may be in one of the many squads that work on a product or service. In the diagram below, point A is when Squad 1 finishes the work. Point B is when Squad 2 finishes their work. If Squad 2's Sprint 3 depends on Squad 1's Sprint 2, then it's ok since Sprint 2 finishes before Sprint 3 is started. But if Squad 2's Sprint 3 depends on Squad 1's Sprint 3, the schedule might not align.

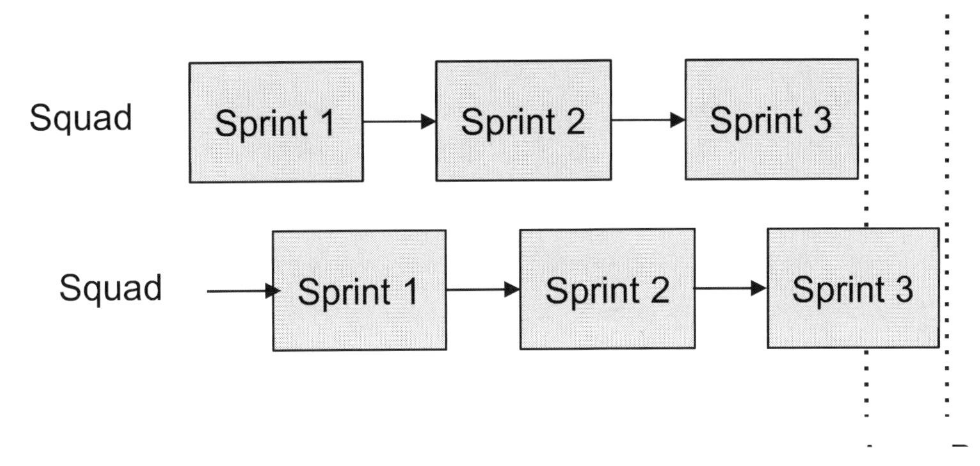

- Before a sprint is worked on, the Squad gets together to decide what to work on next. This is an exercise in prioritizing what should get built in the next sprint and why. The engineers come up with the estimates of the work items and negotiations between members of the Squad occur to determine what items can actually fit into the sprint.

<u>Sample Agile Process (Planning to Finalization of Sprint)</u>

Commence Sprint Planning → Estimate Stories → Prioritize Stories → Finalize Sprint

- Each work item in the sprint (or Story) has an estimate and prioritization and is assigned an engineer.
- An engineer may work on one or more Stories in a sprint.
- An engineer/developer will provide their status at the daily standups, which occur every day or at a frequency that is amenable to the team.
- At the end of the Sprint, it's demo time! Every engineer is expected to demo their work! The code gets pushed to customers (if software is in the cloud) so customers will see the updates almost instantaneously.

<u>Sample Agile Process (During Sprint)</u>

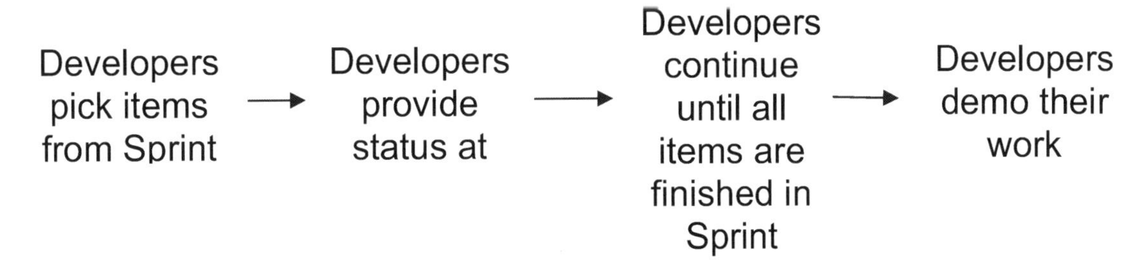

- Feedback from customers is collected. Customer requirements are rewritten, slightly tweaked, or unchanged. Then, the sprint cycle begins again.

Who do you need to do Agile? You need an Agile Scrum Master, which is usually a project or program manager and in some cases the engineering manager. You also need involvement from the Product Manager and the engineers.

Who do you need when you do OOAD? You mostly need yourself, the engineer. You may have questions for the Product Manager and even your boss, but the brunt of it is all on you.

Do you now see the difference between OOAD and Agile? I have just summarized a "roll-up your sleeves"/real-life example of Agile. This process should be a well-oiled machine if done properly. Notice how OOAD is not mentioned in any of the Agile steps!

10.4 OOAD in Agile

Now, let's see how we can embed OOAD into this (or see where OOAD would fit in).

Recall that OOAD is a software design thought process, not a "project management" scheduling process as we saw above. In the above diagrams we detailed how Agile works from sprint planning to defining a sprint, then working on the sprint, and finally re-doing everything again every 2 or 4 weeks depending on how long your sprints are. If you are using Agile or pseudo-Agile (this has been a term getting popularity where not all Agile principles are followed), then you and your team will follow the sprint schedule day-in and day-out.
So where does OOAD fit in? Here's where. The areas below are where OOAD would best fit into Agile. By no means is this an exhaustive list because it will depend on how your company or team implements Agile (or pseudo-Agile), but this list is good enough to give you an idea of what to expect.

- Sprint Planning
    - One of the first steps in creating or working on a Sprint is to plan what work items actually goes into a Sprint. This is where the requirements and use cases are broken down into stories. Each story is a work item that is to be completed by one or more developers. Each story is usually completed in one sprint (and if not, broken down to multiple stories so that a piece at a time can be completed in one sprint).
    - Your job as a developer/engineer is use your OOAD-sense to assert your technical know-how in the planning stage. An example is this:
        - "This module is too large for one sprint, let's break this into multiple modules and create stories for each of the pieces." You need to know, using your OOAD spidery sense and technical know-how, that in fact, the module is large and in fact it should be broken up. Or you can say,
        - "Yea, let's plan this sprint around dividing this module into separate components where each component can be a story or so. We need to do this because we need to satisfy all the high priority requirements and we want to do it in a way that we can demo something at the end of the sprint. So how about we separate these

components further down into a dependency graph and based on that determine how we should tackle this?" This is a much better response to the above, but provides the same message.

- Sprint - Story Estimation
  - Estimating a story is not a difficult task because you are not estimating this, in most cases, by yourself. There is usually at least one other person to provide a "fact-checker" to verify that something is either a small, medium, or large amount of work in order to keep things honest.
  - Your use of OOAD in this task is very similar to the OOAD-spidery-sense you used in the previous example. You need to know the code, how convoluted or not it is and what it would take to modify/add the code to make it work with the existing system.

- During Sprint - Story Design
  - After the sprint has been finalized and you as an engineer are assigned a story to work on, you need to determine how to solve the problem - you do this using straight forward OOAD - what we've been learning this entire book. You need to analyze the story and then start your design. You should come up with UML diagrams, if warranted, and other documents to support your design. Everything that you've learned in this book goes into this part of the Agile process.
  - In an Agile world, documentations are usually in the form of a wiki, but let that company/team dictate what technology to use.

- During Sprint - Story Coding
  - Once you've come up with a design, you need to code it. Again, look at the company/team to see what existing tools that are in use. There are some pretty archaic tools out there and if you find yourself using a tool that slows down or hinders your progress, you should consider making a case to change to different tools. As an example, not all workplaces use StarUML to autogenerate code. They may use Eclipse instead and generate code that way in their specific format. So, you may want to check to see which tool works in what environment because you definitely don't want to use the wrong one and find that you have to do things over again if certain protocol or standards are not followed.

10.5 Wrapping up OOAD and Agile

I hope this chapter provides a practical look into how OOAD is merged with Agile today. The coherence has almost made OOAD and Agile inseparable, but as we have discovered they are both independent on its own and that their combination makes them conducive to each other.

[This page left intentionally blank]

10.6 Exercises

1. What software development methodology do you or have you used in the companies that you worked for?

2. Have you used Agile? If so, what are your thoughts?

3. Compare and contrast Agile and Waterfall methodologies.

4. What do you like about Agile?

5. What are your fears or uncertainties about Agile?

[This page left intentionally blank]

11 EXAMPLE #1 – MONITORING DASHBOARD

Let's apply everything that we've learned in this book to this example that deals with software systems.

11.1 What You Are Provided

Pretend you are given the following brief use cases and mockups at work as follows. Our goal is use the methods learned in this book to convert this brief use case to a UML Class Diagram (and later in the chapter an Architectural Flow Diagram). *Note: in the real world you are likely also given requirements as written in the PRD, but for simplicity, let's assume this is all you are given and that you have already "analyzed" this use case with the product manager.*

> Brief Use Case #1: As a user of the web app, I can monitor my system of servers using a single dashboard that shows me the state of each of my server so that I can take the necessary action to provision additional machines if the CPU utilization of my system is too high. If I see the CPU utilization of one or more machines hit 80%, I can decide to provision (in a separate user interface) additional machines to help with the workload.

Assumptions:

- The web app does not exist, so you are designing the front end as well as the monitoring system backend.
- Assume the "state" of each system is a graph of each server showing the following three attributes: "CPU utilization", "RAM memory usage", and "Bandwidth utilization".
- Assume the graphs are updated in real time.
- There is a separate interface to provision additional machines that you are not responsible for, and as such, not part of your UML design.
- Assume data will be required for the graphs
- 80% is just a number that the user can configure.

Brief Use Case #2: As a user of the web app, I can set alerts of my system of servers using the same monitoring dashboard so that I don't have to keep my eyes glued to the computer screen. I can set alerts for attributes such as "CPU utilization", "RAM memory usage", and "Bandwidth utilization" and configure the actual percentage number that I would like to be

Assumptions:

- The web app is the same web app described in use case #1. You will want to use the same one to also provide alerting feature.

Here are two mockups of the main dashboard and a dialog to create a new alert.

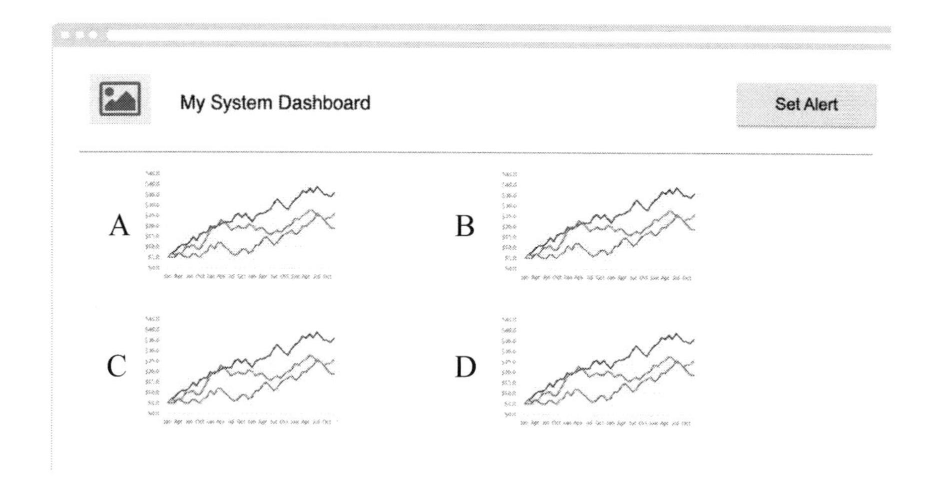

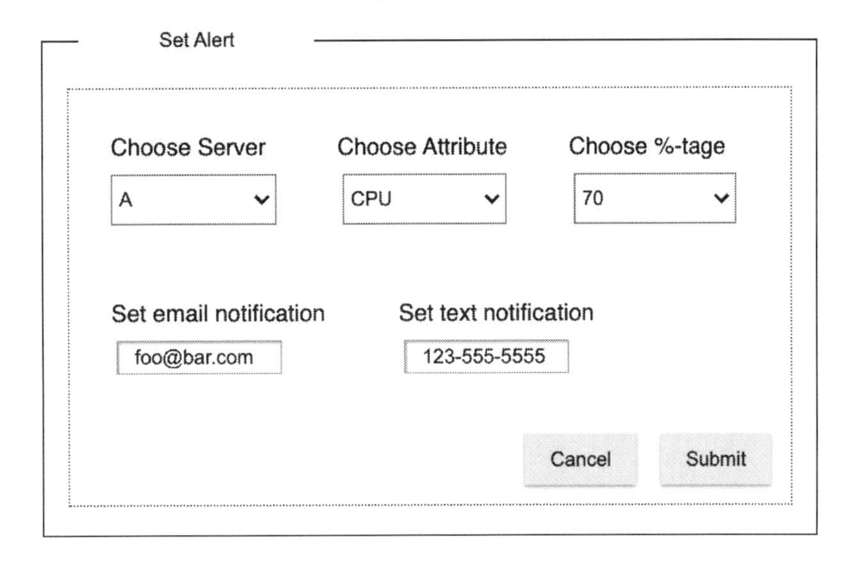

In the above mockup, we see both use cases #1 and #2 come together. This is the mockup of the web app as seen in a web browser. The top part shows a potential image and the name of the dashboard "My System Dashboard". To the right is a button where alerts can be configured. Below the line, there are four graphs shown of four different servers (A, B, C, and D) in the system. There are 3 different lines in each graph, which will represent the 3 different utilization attributes of the server (CPU, Memory, and Bandwidth). The requirements were not clear about the scrolling and pagination, as there could be more graphs we would want to show, so we can ignore those details for now.

11.2 What do we do next?

Remember our goal, we need to come up with UML diagrams. In the ideal situation, we should be coming up with these "in our head", or at least get a good interpretation of what our system looks like in our head and how we think we will build the system. But for now, since we are walking before we run, let's follow the process.

So what do we do next? It is appropriate to use the ABCDFG Method. Recall the Method from Chapter 6 of this book.

We use the **ABCDFG Method** in this order.

1. **A**nalyze the User Flow
2. **B**ox the nouns
3. **C**ircle the verbs
4. **D**ocument other nouns from (A)
5. **F**ilter the candidates
6. **G**raph the relationships

The ABCDFG Method calls for analyzing the user flow as the first step. We did this by drawing a diagram to help us visualize the user flow, but anyway that helps you will work.

> In "Analyze the User Flow", we do two main tasks:
>
> 1. Understand the user flow from start to end
> 2. Understand the inputs and outputs

First, let's make sure we understand the user flow.

The brief use case that was written, ideally, should have been a little bit more explicit and laid out what the user does. Because it doesn't, let's make some assumptions about how the user will use the dashboard. Let's write all this down as we understand it as follows:

- User loads webpage http://dashboard
- User sees the graphs of the servers in his system. The graphs dynamically change based on the data flowing in. The graphs look like they get automatically updated every second.
- User decides to set an alert for a specific server "A" so that he can be alerted when the CPU utilization of "A" hits 90%.
- User clicks on "Set Alert" button and is provided a dialog window to configure the Server, the attribute, and the percentage level to alert on. User can either enter an email address or a phone number for text notification.
- User then clicks on Submit to create the alert.

Now that we more clearly understand the user flow, what are the inputs and outputs? Before you read on, stop, spend a few minutes to think, and write down your answer.

Here's what you should have written:

> The **inputs** of the system are a (1) bunch of machine data and (2) alert configuration from the user.
>
> The **outputs** of the system are (1) configured alerts and (2) graphs.

How did I arrive at the inputs and outputs? Here are some questions to help you: What does the user do? What does the user see and where does it come from? What is the end state?

Let's try to diagram this.

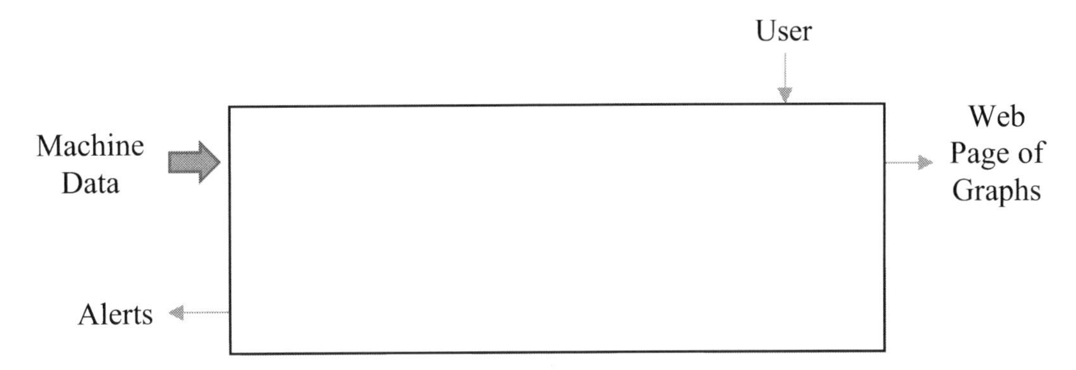

Two inputs, two outputs. The box where the arrows enter and exit is our system that we need to design.

On the next page, we show the nouns and verbs in step A, along with the other steps (B,C) for simplicity.

The next two important steps are to **B**ox the nouns and **C**ircle the verbs. Let's take the user flow that we've written and also the brief use cases provided to us for this combined step.

Boxing the Nouns & Circling the Verbs

Brief Use Case #1: As a user of the web app, I can monitor my system of servers using a single dashboard that shows me the state of each of my server so that I can take the necessary action to provision additional machines if the CPU utilization of my system is too high. If I see the CPU utilization of one or more machines hit 80%, I can decide to provision (in a separate user interface) additional machines to help with the workload.

Brief Use Case #2: As a user of the web app, I can set alerts of my system of servers using the same monitoring dashboard so that I don't have to keep my eyes glued to the computer screen. I can set alerts for attributes such as "CPU utilization", "RAM memory usage", and "Bandwidth utilization" and configure the actual percentage number that I would like to be alerted. I can also configure to get a text message on my phone or an email sent to my inbox.

From our user flow analysis:

- User loads webpage http://dashboard
- User sees the graphs of the servers in his system. The graphs dynamically change based on the data flowing in. The graphs look like they get automatically updated every second.
- User decides to set an alert for a specific server "A" so that he can be alerted when the CPU utilization of "A" hits 90%.
- User clicks on "Set Alert" button and is provided a dialog window to configure the Server, the attribute, and the percentage level to alert on. User can either enter an email address or a phone number for text notification.
- User then clicks on Submit to create the alert.

Here's the list of nouns and verbs we boxed and circled, respectively and combined into Step **D**ocument other nouns.

Candidate Nouns		Candidate Verbs
• User • Webapp • System • Dashboard • State • Server • CPU utilization	• Alerts • RAM • Bandwidth • Graphs • Text • Email • percentage	• Monitor • Shows • Set/configure • Sent • Loads • change

For Step **F**ilter the Candidates, we have to analyze each noun/verb to see if each is going to be a class in our UML class diagram or not.

- User – We don't know anything about the user other than that the user presses buttons. There's no concept of a "stored" state or attributes for the user. Because of these reasons, user is not a class in our UML class diagram.
- Web app and dashboard are essentially the same thing. A dashboard is a collection of graphs and buttons. Because of this "collection of" relationship that dashboard has with other candidates, we say that dashboard is a class.
- For system, this is a little bit nuanced, but a system is a collection of servers. Furthermore, a dashboard shows the state of the system, so there is a 1:1 relationship. Therefore, system is a class.
- By state, we mean the utilization of each of the attributes (CPU, RAM, BW). This appears to be a value, rather than a class that would hold multiple attributes.
- For server, as we discussed in system, a server has the three attributes. So it looks like state as we discussed above, is an attribute of server.
- For CPU utilization, RAM, and Bandwidth, we discuss these together since they are all the same, just different forms of the same type. They each hold a single value, which is a percentage, so they are not classes.
- An alert is a class because it's a representation of an entity that includes what to alert on.
- A graph is a collection of data points so it is a class.
- Text and email are different forms of the same thing. They can be classes (or attributes); if they are classes then we can create a superclass to represent them as "ContactInfo" or we can keep them as attributes so all they store is a string of alphanumeric characters; it's your choice.
- Percentage is a value, not a class.

Class Nouns	
• System • Dashboard • Server • Alerts	• Graphs • ContactInfo • Text • email

Before we graph, which is our last step, let's take a look at the verbs.

- The user monitors, not the system, so it's not an operation in any class.
- The "shows" (or display) operation is what is displayed on the screen. We can embed this operation in the Graph class. This way, the dashboard will call each Graph class to "show" the graph.
- Set/configure alerts is definitely an operation in the Dashboard class because the Dashboard creates them and stores the alerts.
- Sent is an operation, but it doesn't fit neatly into any of the above nouns. Are we missing a class? In our current model, it looks like there is no concept of "triggering" an alert. We can add this in to Dashboard, but then the Dashboard will be responsible for alerting, or we can have a separate class, whose job it is to look at the triggers created by the Dashboard, checks them regularly, checks the data coming in, and fires any alerts to the user. So it looks like it makes sense to add another class!

Class Nouns	
• System • Dashboard • Server • Alerts	• Graphs • ContactInfo • Text • Email • AlertTrigger

The final step is to **Graph**. Here is one example of what the UML class diagram would look like. The associations between each class are examples only, and they will depend on how you classify each of the associations. The attributes and operations of each class are also incomplete, but in general, this is what your UML class diagram should approximately look like.

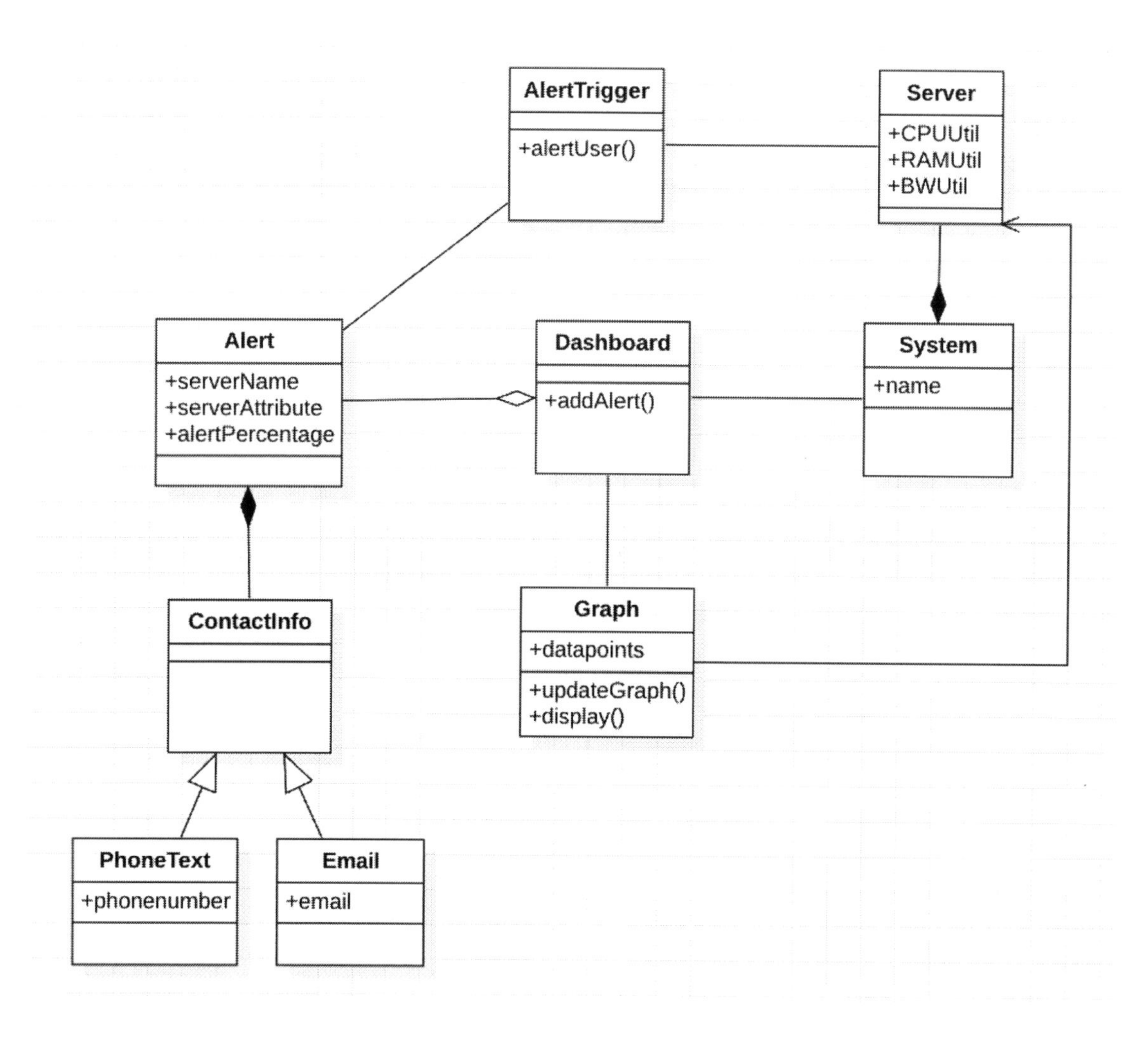

So are we done? Well, while we did achieve our goal of creating a UML class diagram from a bunch of use cases that we analyzed, it would be even better to also expand upon the input/output diagram that we drew earlier. Specifically, I want to know what is supposed to go *inside* that box! We drew the precursor to an AFD, so let's complete it!

Here's one interpretation of what the AFD should approximately look like. As the machine data from the servers are coming in, the data needs to be collected and stored. The stored data goes to be displayed on the dashboard (Web Page of Graphs). When an alert is created, the AlertTrigger module is responsible for alerting the user.

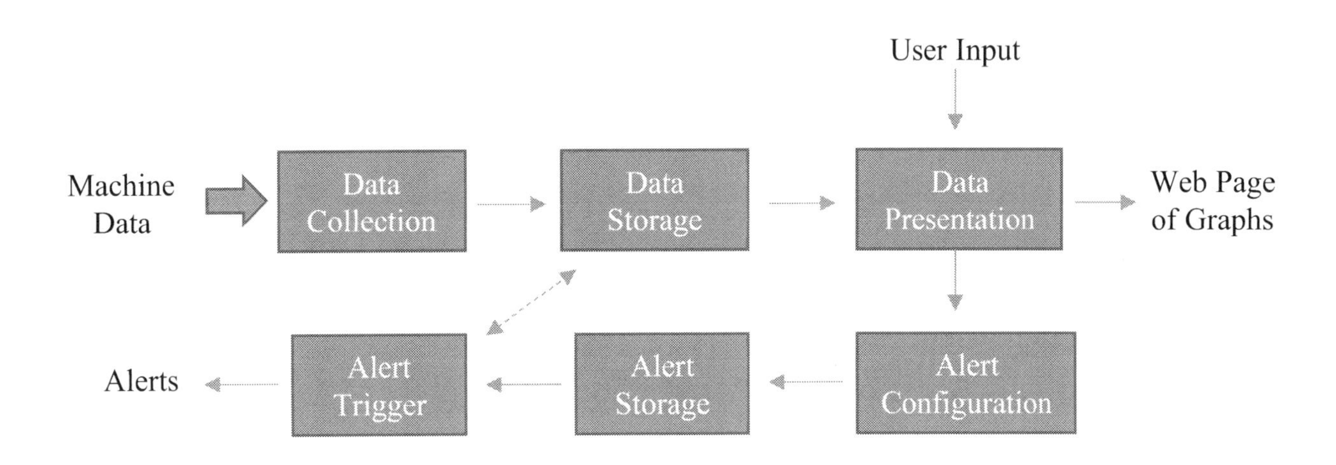

So there you have them! A UML Class Diagram and an AFD!

[This page left intentionally blank]

UML Class Diagram Cheat Sheet

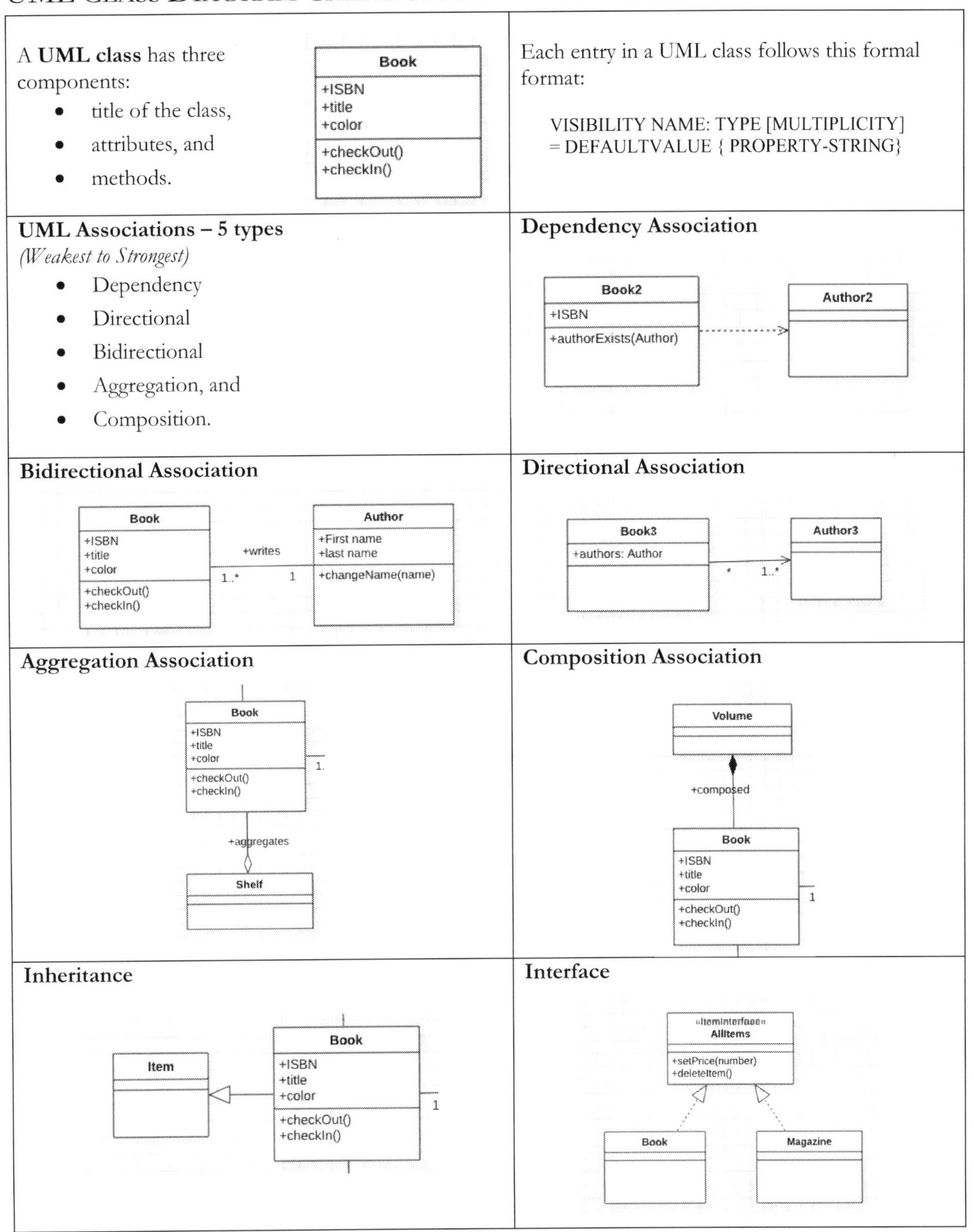

[This page left intentionally blank]

UML SEQUENCE DIAGRAM CHEAT SHEET

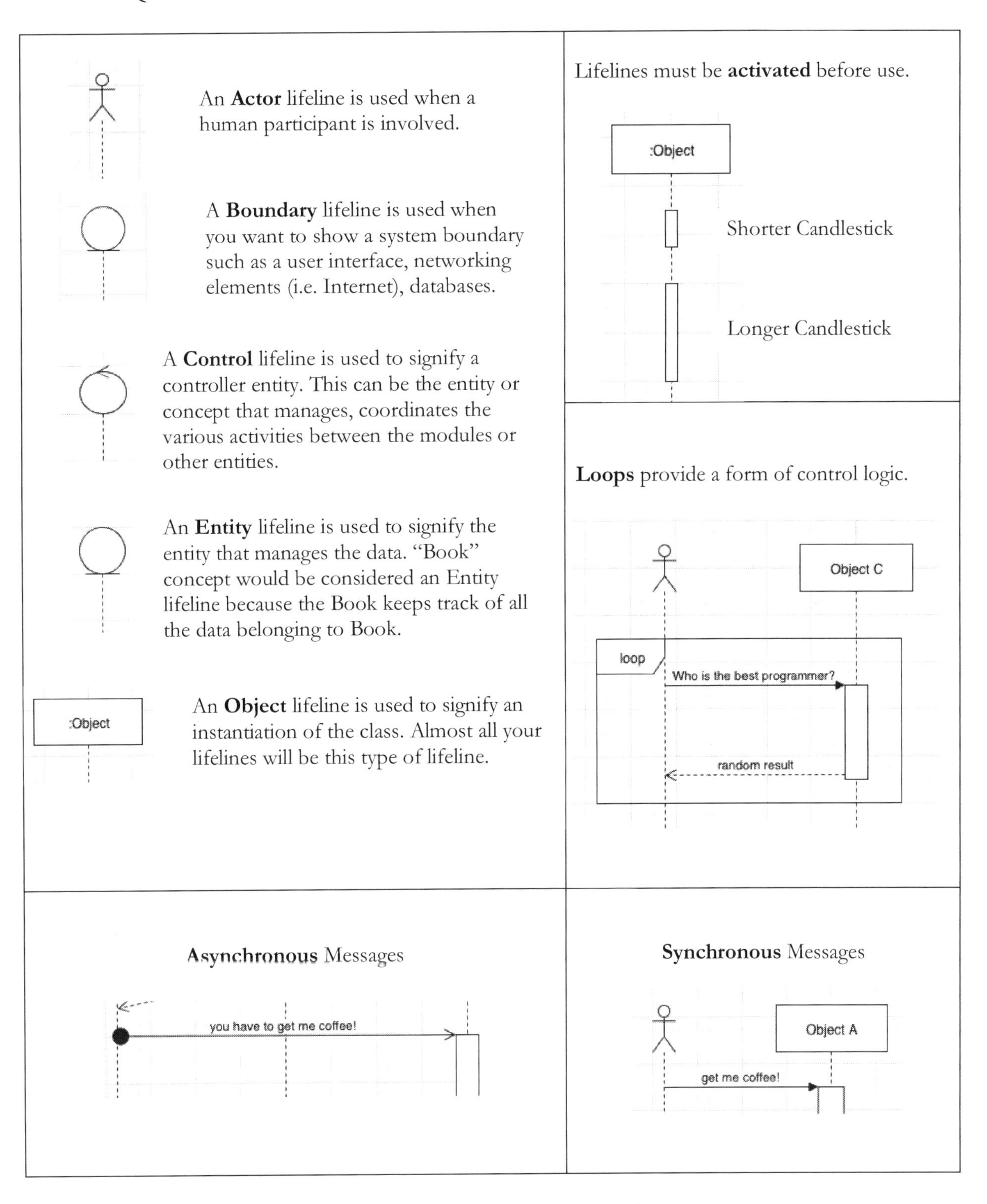

[This page left intentionally blank]

INDEX

[This page left intentionally blank]

REFERENCES

This book stands on the shoulders of giants – computer scientists of the world who helped shape software engineering to what it is today.

Attribution has been given to those in the footnotes throughout the book.

Additional Readings:

- GRASP Principles – Craig Larman's Applying UML and Patterns 3rd Edition
- UML Distilled, Martin Fowler
- Design Patterns, Gang of Four

I would also like to thank the professors/advisors who I had at UC Berkeley and UCLA who gave me the opportunity to work with or for them and who I deeply learned a lot from.

2ND DEDICATION

The author would like to thank Andy Hou (Retired Director of Engineering Department at the University of California) for giving him the opportunity to impart his knowledge to students all around the world and his suggestion to write a book for my class. Thank you Andy and I hope you realize your dream of traveling the world in your RV.

[This page left intentionally blank]

ABOUT THE AUTHOR

Edwin Mach has been teaching computer science for over a decade. He graduated from UC Berkeley with a B.A. in Computer Science and UCLA with a M.S. in Computer Science.

One of the highly rated classes he teaches is Object Oriented Analysis and Design at the University of California campus, where he had held off writing his own textbook for 10 years until he got the courage (and student and admin prodding) to write his own. International students from all over the world have taken his course (i.e. Japan, Brazil, South Korea, Indonesia).

He enjoys the outdoors with his family in sunny California.

[This page left intentionally blank]

Got Feedback?

Email the author at ooadcookbook@gmail.com

Selected Feedback for Edwin's OOAD Course

(Responses were anonymous and conducted by University of California. They are copied here verbatim and where clarity needed "[…]" is used. These are some of the comments made by students over the past few classes that I am most proud of or shine a light into the concepts taught in class.)

"Professor Mach embodies all of the qualities an excellent instructor must have: patience, pedagogical prowess, responsiveness, and a firm grasp of the subject matter."

"We did a lot of exercises on the class, and they are awesome!"

"[He has the] ability to shape classroom discussion based on responses of student[s]. Knew when to divert from book topic to industry best practice"

"The course provided a very solid introduction to and summary of various OOAD concepts, at a level deep enough to be useful and practical, but not so deep as to be impenetrable or unapproachable. The ABCDFG method was particularly useful – despite seeming a bit simplistic or contrived when first introduced."

Made in the USA
Middletown, DE
16 February 2023